AN INVENTORY
FOR THE NATION

RCAHMS

Published in 2015 by the
Royal Commission on the Ancient and Historical
Monuments of Scotland (RCAHMS)
John Sinclair House · 16 Bernard Terrace
Edinburgh EH8 9NX

telephone +44 (0)131 662 1456
info@rcahms.gov.uk · www.rcahms.gov.uk

Registered Charity SC026749

British Library Cataloguing-in-Publication Data. A catalogue
record for this book is available from the British Library.

ISBN 978 1 902419 97 8

Crown Copyright © RCAHMS 2015

Written by James Crawford
Research by Philip Brooks, Richard Sobolewski
and James Crawford.

Typeset in Futura and Bodoni
Printed in Scotland by McAllister Litho Glasgow

Cover: Pirnmill, Arran, 2008. DP056902
Back: C S T Calder at Dun An Ruigh Ruadh, 1954. SC1121381

An Inventory for the Nation

Royal Commission on the Ancient and Historical Monuments of Scotland

FINAL REPORT *of* THE ROYAL COMMISSION ON THE ANCIENT & HISTORICAL MONUMENTS OF SCOTLAND 1908–2015

To the Queen's most excellent Majesty

May it please your Majesty

WE, YOUR MAJESTY'S COMMISSIONERS, appointed to provide for the survey and recording of ancient and historical monuments and constructions connected with, or illustrative of, the contemporary culture, civilisation and conditions of the life of the people in *Scotland* from the earliest times, by compiling, maintaining and curating the national record of the archaeological and historical environment; by identifying, surveying, interpreting and recording all buildings, sites and ancient monuments of archaeological, architectural and historical interest in *Scotland*; by providing advice and information relevant to the preservation and conservation of such buildings, sites and ancient monuments of archaeological, architectural and historical interest; by promoting the public use of this information by all appropriate means; and by establishing and maintaining national standards in surveying, recording and curating, and providing guidance on these matters to others, hereby deliver our final report, setting out how, over the past 107 years, we have carried out your Majesty's intentions.

OUR WORK has always been driven by an idea – in its simplest form, that the built and historic environment of *Scotland* must be recorded and researched to ensure that its exceptional cultural value is understood and protected by current and future generations. This Report, our last as a Royal Commission, documents how we have pursued this idea for over a century. It shows how our methods have changed and evolved along with the world around us, tracking the major social and political upheavals that have accompanied two World Wars and the onset of a new millennium. It follows how we have responded and adapted to major technological advances, from the motorcar and powered flight to digital photography and the internet. And it explains how the idea that led to our formation has grown from a vision pursued by a handful of experts to the permanent and enduring work of a national institution: work that, in 2014, was enshrined and protected in legislation passed by the Scottish Parliament.

YOUR COMMISSIONERS are therefore pleased to report that, while our appointment on your Majesty's behalf has come to an end, the task that you set us *never will*.

SIGNED:

PROFESSOR JOHN R. HUME, CHAIRMAN   DIANA MURRAY, SECRETARY, CHIEF EXECUTIVE

The First Report

On the morning of 4 August 1908, Alexander Ormiston Curle, the first Secretary of the Royal Commission on the Ancient and Historical Monuments of Scotland, set off by bicycle from the small village of Coldingham in Berwickshire, travelled through the even smaller village of Ayton, and rode up the steep incline of a rough road leading to Lamberton Moor. He carried with him a canvas bag holding his notebooks, a clinometer and a measuring tape. Strapped to the top bar of his bicycle were his surveyors' rods. At around midday, he passed a copse of trees known as Tam's Wood, and stopped to consult his 6-inches-to-the-mile Ordnance Survey map, which he had backed with linen to make it more durable. Hiding his bicycle carefully behind a wall, he continued on foot to the summit. Once there, he assembled his equipment, and began to take measurements. The hill was crowned by a structure that was over 2,000 years old — Habchester fort, first built in the Iron Age.

A O Curle with camera outside 8 South Learmonth Gardens, Edinburgh in 1932. SC1471043

'Though one half has been entirely obliterated it is still a most striking fort, with two ramparts', wrote Curle in his journal. 'I made use for the first time my surveyor's staff and clinometer and found them both most handy', he continued, going on to record that 'the height of the inner rampart from the foot of the ditch I found to be 12 feet – that of the outer rampart 10 feet and the depth of the outer ditch 6 feet 6 inches ... The defences measure 78 feet overall from the crest of the inner rampart to the top of the counterscarp. The ramparts are of earth and stone.'

From Habchester, he cycled on by an 'execrable road' to Lamberton old church, which was overgrown with weeds, but contained 'nothing of interest'. After a chance meeting with a local woman, he was directed along a path used by the postman to the village of Mordington. Inspecting an old stone 'vault', surrounded by nettles higher than his head, Curle discovered an inscription, which he tried to record by rubbing grass on the paper he had used to wrap his sandwiches. That evening, after returning to St Abbs by bicycle and a short train journey, he wrote in his journal that he had cycled '24 miles and did not feel the least tired when I got in, though I never rested for more than 10 minutes, and that only once when I ate my lunch in a cottage at Lamberton'.

A visitor inspects Habchester Fort. This photograph was taken during the Commission's second survey of Berwickshire in 1915, by James Hewat Craw, a local man who had provided assistance in the identification of sites. SC1096822

'This has been a glorious day – with bright sunshine and a tempering breeze. My walk over the moor and my bicycle ride in the forenoon, were most exhilarating. The bloom of the heather is gone and the brackens have turned a rusty red.'

A O Curle, *The Private Journal of a Wandering Antiquary*, 1908

Two days earlier, on 2 August, Curle had begun what he described as his 'course of inspection of all the ancient monuments of Scotland'. His first day was spent exploring the coast to the south of St Abbs – where he was staying for a month with his family in the Anchorage Inn – but he found nothing that met his criteria for recording. On his second day, after another fruitless search in the fishing village of Eyemouth, he cycled some three miles to a place called Chester Hill, marked on his Ordnance Survey map with the enigmatic title of 'site'. Here, he wrote, was the first place that 'justified greater attention'. With the assistance of a young farm boy, he made a 'rapid survey'. While Curle doubted the accuracy of his measurements, he resolved that they were, at least, 'better than the word "site"'. They were also significant. This was the first ever 'survey' in the history of the Royal Commission. His more meticulous work at Habchester, the following day, was the second.

Curle continued throughout August, September and October of 1908. On 7 November, his work was finally complete. 'And so ends my first experience as the wandering antiquary of the Ancient Monuments Commission', he wrote. 'I have inspected over 200 objects in Berwickshire, and written up notes on them. My bicycle has carried me almost 300

Habchester pictured during a Royal Commission survey flight in 2001. SC993205

miles; five times only have I hired a trap and twice a motor car, the number of miles I have tramped by moorland and meadow I have no reckoning of but they are many. It has never been anything but the most intense pleasure to me.'

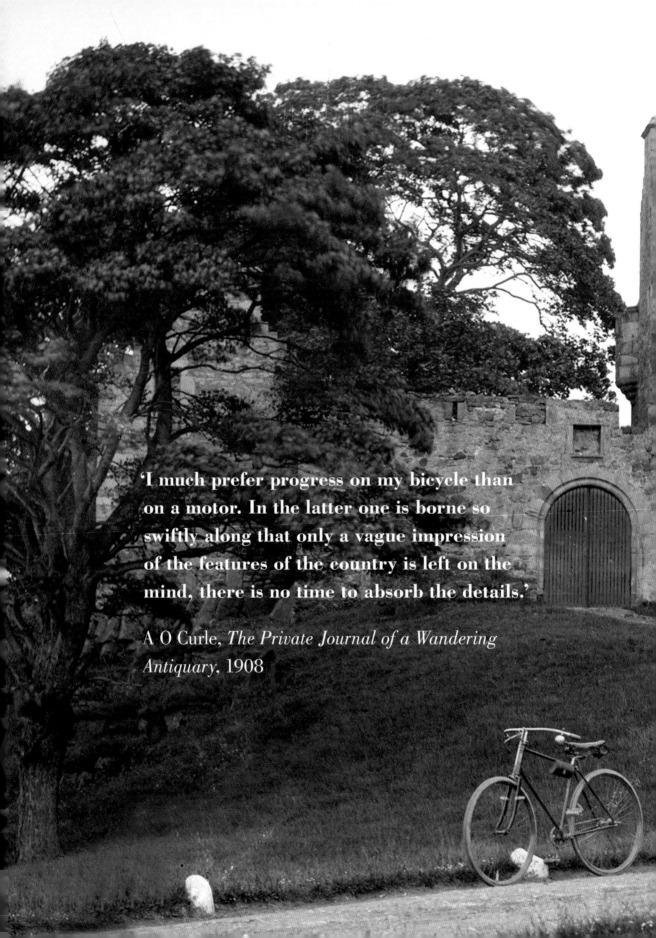

'I much prefer progress on my bicycle than on a motor. In the latter one is borne so swiftly along that only a vague impression of the features of the country is left on the mind, there is no time to absorb the details.'

A O Curle, *The Private Journal of a Wandering Antiquary*, 1908

In 1909, Curle's work was published as the *First Report and Inventory of Monuments and Constructions of the Royal Commission* – a report prepared for King Edward VII and presented to both Houses of Parliament 'by Command of His Majesty'. It contained notes of 260 sites, of which 70 were previously unknown, and it listed 51 as being most worthy of preservation: split into 48 not in 'imminent risk of demolition or decay', and 3 in immediate need of protection. In the introduction to the report, it was noted that 'it is very gratifying to your Commissioners to state that your Majesty's Commission has everywhere been fully appreciated and favourably received, and that the greatest assistance has been given to your Commissioners in carrying out the work which you have entrusted them'. Encouraged by this early progress, they continued by proposing 'in the current year to review the monuments in the county of Sutherland, and also, if possible, those in the County of Caithness'. The work of creating an inventory of the nation had begun.

Granton Castle, c1915. SC581331

A National Inventory, by Royal Command

The first meeting of the Royal Commission was held at No. 29 St Andrews Square, Edinburgh, at 3pm on 26 February 1908. In attendance were the Secretary, Alexander Curle, the Chairman, Sir Herbert Maxwell, and the six Commissioners, Lord Charles Guthrie, Professor Gerard Baldwin Brown, William T Oldrieve, Frances C Buchanan, Thomas H Bryce and W Thomas Ross. Almost three weeks earlier, on 7 February, the Royal Commission had been inaugurated formally. It was tasked, by Letters Patent of Edward VII, with making 'an inventory of the Ancient and Historical Monuments and Constructions connected with or illustrative of the contemporary culture, civilisation and conditions of life of the people in Scotland from earliest times to the year 1707' and 'to specify those which seem most worthy of preservation'. Examples were given of the type of structures that this might include – stone circles or standing stones; forts, camps, earthworks, brochs and crannogs; and architectural structures, 'ecclesiastical or secular, whether ruinous or in use'. Crucially, however, what was absent was any indication of exactly *how* the Commission should go about its work.

29 St Andrew's Square photographed by Henry Bedford Lemere in 1903. SC730049

It was this question that dominated the proceedings of the meeting. To begin with, they resolved that they would consult Ordnance Survey maps of all of Scotland – at the scale of 6 inches to the mile – to make a series of lists, ordered by county and parish, of all the monuments that had been recorded. To capture sites that did not appear on the maps, the lists would be reviewed and updated, drawing on relevant information found in books and research works, and the expert knowledge of the Commissioners themselves. Finally, the lists would be sent out to 'ministers of the Gospel, schoolmasters and such other individuals as might be able to supplement these lists from local knowledge'. The minutes were still a little coy, however, on the next step. 'Hereafter a more detailed inventory is to be undertaken' in order to produce a 'general description' of each monument, 'drawing attention to its characteristic features and noting any peculiarities observable'.

The First Report of 1909 clarified exactly what the Commissioners meant when they recommended a 'more detailed inventory'. It was, they said, 'considered essential that the Secretary should visit each county in turn, with the object of personally inspecting each monument as to satisfy your Commissioners as to its true character and condition'.

Watercolour of Clach a' Charra standing stone in the western Highlands, from the Society of Antiquaries collection. This painting dates from the late nineteenth century, and was the work of the artist and antiquarian James Drummond. SC110830

This was not a task, they declared, that could be carried out satisfactorily by just poring over maps and leafing through books. For the inventory to have any real value, the Royal Commission had to go out into the field to see the nation's ancient structures with its own eyes. This decision, taken within the first hour of the organisation's professional existence, shaped its entire history for the next 107 years.

'It was also considered essential that the Secretary should visit each county in turn, with the object of personally inspecting each monument as to satisfy your Commissioners as to its true character and condition.'

First Report and Inventory of Monuments and Constructions in the County of Berwick, 1909

The meeting on 26 February had looked to devise a practical response to a more philosophical idea: that the fragments and traces of the past remaining within the modern landscape were innately precious and valuable. At the beginning of the twentieth century, this idea was both new and novel. It was only in 1869 that the prospect of the State protection of 'national monuments' was raised in the House of Commons, and it took another four years for a bill to be introduced. Even then, it was not until almost a decade later, in 1882, that the concept was ratified in the first Ancient Monuments Protection Act. This Act set out powers for the government's Commissioners of Works to assume the responsibility of caring for a defined number of sites – although still subject to the agreement of the owners on whose land they were situated. Almost a third of all the monuments deemed most important in the United Kingdom were in Scotland. At that time, however, this amounted to just 21 structures.

Nevertheless, the Act contained the kernel of the idea that would drive the future Royal Commission: that ancient monuments were tangible elements of national memory, and their loss would impact fundamentally on the richness of a country's collective cultural heritage. The 1882 Act, although very limited in scope, provided a crucial first legal recognition that historical physical structures should be protected and conserved. It was also part of a wider academic step-change: the passion-pursuit of antiquarianism was evolving into the professional specialism of archaeology. Increasingly, people questioned the basis of the list provided by the 1882 Act. How accurate could it be, when there had never been any systematic national survey of Britain's sites and monuments?

'What is wanted is a survey of all monuments of antiquity of every kind.'

David Murray, *An Archaeological Survey of the United Kingdom*, 1896

In 1896, the Glasgow lawyer and antiquarian David Murray published *An Archaeological Survey of the United Kingdom*. It was not, despite its title, an actual survey, but a call to action for the government to identify definitively 'all monuments of antiquity of every kind, for example, pillar stones and cromlechs, circles and alignments, cairns and barrows, camps, forts and other earthworks, crosses, wells, churches and graveyards, crannogs, peels, castles, and other buildings, the sites where the buildings are gone, caves, cup and ring-marked rocks, British and Celtic trackways, and Roman roads'. He continued that the results of the survey should be used to update all Ordnance Survey maps, and should also be compiled in regional reports 'containing a concise description of each object and exact details of its size, position, and the like, and a scale-plan or section in the case of the more important, and, where necessary, a photograph and measured drawing'. Just under a decade later, in 1905, Gerard Baldwin Brown,

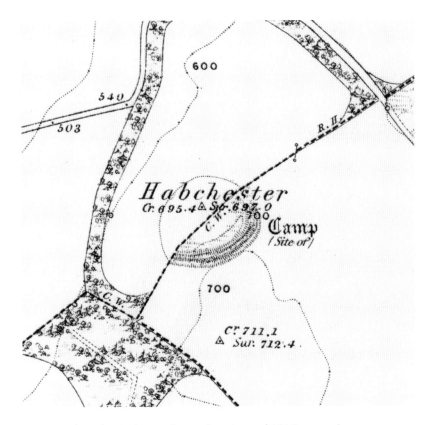

An extract from the Ordnance Survey 1st edition of 1860, centred on Habchester fort. DP221438.

Professor of Fine Art at the University of Edinburgh and a future Commissioner of the Royal Commission, published a book called *The Care of Ancient Monuments*. Restating Murray's belief that a comprehensive survey was essential, Baldwin Brown continued that 'if ever a national work of inventorisation were set on foot, it is in Scotland that it might be started with the best promise of a satisfactory result'.

As it turned out, it *was* in Scotland that the survey began. After reading Baldwin Brown's book, the new Secretary of State for Scotland, Sir John Sinclair, became an enthusiastic convert to the cause. He proposed setting up a Royal Commission, a process begun in February 1907, and completed a year later, with the appointment of a Chairman – Sir Herbert Maxwell, President of the Society of Antiquaries of Scotland – six Commissioners, and a Secretary. This last post was, in many respects, the most important. While the Commissioners were there to advise, and sometimes contribute to surveys, the burden of the work would fall on the Secretary. Curle was considered the perfect candidate: a forty-one-year-old solicitor, he was also a passionate and prolific antiquarian, had published a number of papers in the *Proceedings of the Society of Antiquaries of Scotland*, and, in 1905, had been elected as co-Secretary of the Society. Two more Royal Commissions on Ancient Monuments were established in the same year – in Wales in August, and England in October – by which time Curle was already criss-crossing Berwickshire by bicycle with his map, compass, measuring rods and notebook.

Curle worked at a remarkable pace, sometimes spending over half a year in the field. He began his second

Tongue, Sutherland, the second County to be surveyed by the Commission, photographed here by Erskine Beveridge, a mill owner and antiquarian in 1886. SC1113115

survey, of Sutherland, in May 1909. This was an altogether different proposition to gliding from village to village along the undulating roads and tracks of Berwickshire. Sutherland, occupying the most north-westerly corner of the British mainland, was remote and rugged, a landscape of mountains and lochs, wide, desolate moorlands, and long, serrated coastlines. Curle worked throughout the summer and the autumn, basing himself at a number of different rented houses and hotels across the county. Local knowledge, so much a feature of the first inventory, was scant by comparison. As the introduction to the *Second Report and Inventory of Monuments and Constructions in the County of Sutherland* explained, 'owing to the great extent of the county and the sparseness of its population, trustworthy information regarding its ancient monuments was difficult to obtain'.

As a result, Curle's work in the region was truly pioneering. 'The monuments and constructions of Sutherland', explained the Report, 'were found greatly to exceed in number and importance those previously known to exist'. This second field survey also discovered a worrying trend, which would go on to have major implications for the future of the Commission's work. 'We view with much regret', continued the introduction, 'the destruction which has overtaken so many

'We believe that there still exist a certain number of objects which have not come under our observation.'

Second Report and Inventory of Monuments and Constructions in the County of Sutherland, 1911

remarkable prehistoric monuments and constructions throughout the county owing to the facilities they have afforded for a supply of stones for road-metal and building purposes', and 'the practice of planting trees upon or immediately adjacent to them'. Curle's *Second Report* was published in 1911, and ran to 195 pages – 136 pages longer than Berwickshire. On the one hand, it highlighted the importance of the Commission's work, creating, for the first time, an official record of a large number of previously unknown sites or structures. Yet, on the other, it provided an early intimation of the true, yawning scale of the task at hand. A 'National Inventory' had the potential to be vastly greater than anyone had previously foreseen. As the *Second Report* admitted, rather matter-of-factly, 'we believe that there still exist a certain number of objects which have not come under our observation'.

Nevertheless, while each subsequent Report was larger than the last, Curle continued his rapid yet methodical progress through the surveys. He moved from Sutherland to Caithness, Wigtownshire and Kirkcudbrightshire. This remarkable work-rate was only halted by his decision, in June 1913, to resign as Secretary to take up the position of Director of the National Museum of Antiquities. Even then, he was appointed instantly as a Commissioner, continued to provide assistance in field surveys to subsequent Secretaries, and remained in his advisory post until his retirement in 1951.

In March 1916, the work of the Commission was suspended until the end of the First World War. In its first eight years, a great deal had been achieved. Five of the twenty-five county inventories had been published – while two more field surveys had been completed. By that measure, all of Scotland would be covered – and all of the Commission's work completed – by the midpoint of the twentieth century.

A O Curle in his drawing room c1923. SC371006

National Rescue

In June 1945, British Army Captain Kenneth Steer was appointed to the North Rhine Division of the Monuments, Fine Arts and Archives programme (MFAA). Along with some 400 other serviceman and civilians, he was tasked with safeguarding historical and cultural monuments, art and antiquities from war damage. The 'Monuments Men', as the staff of the programme were nicknamed, began their work in 1943, and continued beyond the end of the conflict, up to the midpoint of 1946. After the fighting had ceased, their task was to oversee repairs to damaged structures, and to search out, recover, catalogue and store priceless artworks. Before the Second World War, Steer had been the Assistant Archaeologist of the Royal Commission. In 1941, he was called up to work in Military Intelligence, and between 1943 and 1945, he was the head of the Air Photographic Interpretation Unit of the 56th Division, working on the Allied landing campaign in Italy. During his time with the MFAA his primary responsibility was to secure appropriate building materials to carry out emergency conservation work on the most endangered monuments and structures, including the heavily bomb-damaged medieval cathedral of Cologne.

Cologne, with its great cathedral rising above the smoke, from a 1944 image from the National Collection of Aerial Photography. NCAP 106G 3430 4139

Steer returned to his post at the Royal Commission in the latter half of 1946. He had witnessed at extreme close quarters what war could do to cultural heritage – and he knew that the threat came not just from bombs and bullets. Global conflict set in motion a process of mobilisation and militarisation with the capacity to transform entire national landscapes, and impact fundamentally on the structures – and history – they contained. This impact was felt before arms were taken up, and long after the last shot was fired. As a reaction to the German naval blockade and its attempt to starve Britain of resources, both the wartime and post-war governments looked to pursue a series of policies aimed at guaranteeing future self-sufficiency. In particular, the focus was on food, timber and energy. This saw concerted attempts to claim more and more acreage – termed 'marginal land' – for agricultural production; to increase rapidly the density of national forestry; and to build dams and flood valleys as part of a massive scheme aimed at capturing hydroelectric power. Given the pace and scale of change – and the threat it presented – Steer lobbied for an immediate and countrywide emergency survey of endangered monuments. In a meeting held in November 1949, the Commissioners endorsed Steer's plans. By the spring of 1950, work was underway on what was called the 'Marginal Land Survey'. To explain the importance of the project, the then Secretary Angus Graham wrote an open letter published in *The Times*, *The Scotsman* and the *Glasgow Herald*. By the end of the same year, all other archaeological survey activities of the Royal Commission had ceased.

'The war brought special risks to ancient monuments in all parts of Scotland, not only through enemy action but through the field training of troops, and we endeavoured to forestall such damage by preparing emergency records.'

An Inventory of the Ancient and Historical Monuments of the City of Edinburgh, 1951

As the Commissioners subsequently explained, focusing resources became a necessity: 'Earthworks and forts, apart from those situated on unprofitable hilltops, are subject to constant attrition through ploughing, drainage and other forms of rural exploitation, and this process must be expected to extend as more land is made available for production of food or timber.' As a result, realising that 'rigorous measures should be taken at once to record and, where appropriate, to investigate monuments which must necessarily be destroyed during the next few years, we postponed, at the end of 1950, our normal programme of County Inventories in favour of an emergency survey of marginal lands in all parts of Scotland'.

The concept of a survey *in extremis* was not entirely new to the Commission. During the war, Graham had undertaken a programme of emergency photography in areas of Scotland that were still to be covered by the Commission Inventories – recording, in particular, those historic buildings considered most at risk from enemy attacks. In a climate of suspicion and heightened security, this was not an activity that passed without notice. While photographing Bridge of Don – with a German Leica camera no less – Graham was arrested as a spy and held in a police cell while his identity was checked. Despite such unusual obstacles, by the latter half of 1942, he had produced over 2,300 photographs. From

The Leica III camera purchased in 1938. DP208553

1942 into 1943, this work became even more focussed. Vere Gordon Childe – Professor of Archaeology at the University of Edinburgh and a newly-appointed Commissioner – volunteered to carry out a survey of monuments in military training areas across Scotland. Large tracts of the country had been annexed by the Army and Royal Air Force, with the scale of troop movements and staff and vehicle accommodation alone putting considerable strain on the fabric of the landscape. The use of a chambered cairn for target practice by a Polish artillery company provided a rather dramatic illustration of the risks: archaeology was quite literally in the firing line. Graham and Childe carried out the survey, sometimes together, travelling across Scotland in Graham's car. By the end of 1943, they had identified and recorded some 636 ancient monuments and sites within the training areas.

So Steer's plan did have some precedent. What was unusual, however – particularly given that the post-war Commission was back up to its full complement of staff – was the decision to pursue the emergency survey as a priority above almost everything else. The nature of the work remained clearly within the remit of 'making an inventory'. But it also added a proactive urgency that – at least outside of conflict – was entirely new.

'This threat can be met only by the immediate employment of stereoscopic photographs to identify all unrecorded monuments.'

Kenneth Steer, Memorandum to Commissioners, 1949

What was also new was how the survey was being carried out. From his experiences in Photographic Interpretation during the war, Steer was keenly aware of the value of aerial imagery as a source of information. If multiple aerial images were taken in quick succession – with each overlapping by at least 60 per cent with the one before and the one after – and then viewed through a stereoscope, they resolved into a detailed three-dimensional model, offering the perception of depth and elevation. Stereoscopy was a technology dating from Victorian times, seen at first as something of a parlour trick. Once photography and powered flight were combined in the First and Second World Wars, however, it was employed on a staggering, military-industrial scale. In the context of intelligence-gathering, it played the key role in everything from the preparations for the D-Day landings to the

A stereoscope for interpretation of aerial photography.

hunt for the Nazis' devastating 'V' weapons. In peace-time, however, Steer saw huge potential in its use as a tool for examining the landscapes of the past. From above, patterns could emerge hinting at ancient man-made structures that would have been entirely undetectable from the ground.

Between 1944 and 1950, the RAF conducted a national survey of Scotland, producing stereoscopic aerial photography at a scale of 1:10,000. Steer recommended using this survey – along with other RAF imagery dating back to the 1930s – as the starting point for the Commission's investigations into Marginal Land. First, they would use the imagery to undertake a rapid, landscape-wide assessment to highlight potential new discoveries. This initial sweep would then pinpoint locations for staff to explore in greater detail through ground-checking and field survey – which, after the acquisition of an ex-army jeep, could be carried out in a four-wheel-drive vehicle for the first time. It did not take long for Steer to demonstrate the impact of this approach. Focussing on Berwickshire, scene of the very first county Report, he identified 50 sites that were worthy of further investigation. None of them had been known about before – overlooked by, or indeed invisible to, earlier surveys. Similarly, the study of stereoscopic imagery of Roxburghshire and Selkirkshire

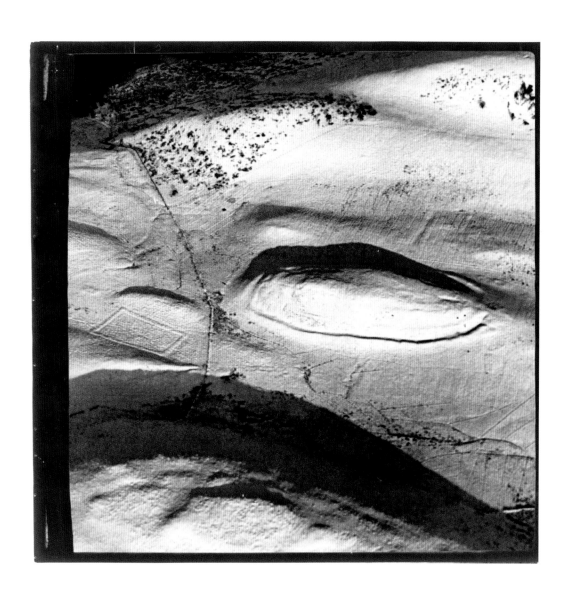

1930 RAF photograph of Maiden Castle Fort in the Lomond Hills –
one of the first aerial photographs published in a County Inventory to
aid interpretation of a monument. SC1123653

demonstrated, as Steer explained, 'that less than two-thirds of the visible monuments in these counties have been previously recorded on the Ordnance Survey maps or in archaeological literature'. In the context of producing a National Inventory, the implications were considerable. 'It is reasonable to assume' wrote Steer, 'that this proportion of unrecorded to recorded monuments holds good for other Scottish counties, including those already surveyed by the Commission'.

'Less than two-thirds of the visible monuments in these counties have been previously recorded ... It is reasonable to assume that this proportion of unrecorded to recorded monuments holds good for other Scottish counties, including those already surveyed by the Commission.'

Kenneth Steer, Memorandum to Commissioners, 1949

It is no exaggeration to say that aerial photography revolutionised the process of archaeological survey. It demonstrated, in compelling and definitive fashion, how technological advancement could open new routes to discovery, and increase comprehensively existing knowledge and understanding.

What it also recalled was a key phrase from the Commission's Second Report on Sutherland, produced four decades earlier: 'we believe that there still exist a certain number of objects which have not come under our observation'.

This sentiment – that sites could be missed and Inventories therefore incomplete – had, in one respect or another, pervaded the Commission's work almost from the very start: and certainly since it had resumed its task in the aftermath of the First World War. The first half of the 1920s was a lean time in the organisation's life, as the government cut its budget and considered postponing its operations 'to a more favourable opportunity'. Between 1919 and 1929, only four Reports were published: for Dumfries; East Lothian; the Outer Hebrides, Skye and the Small Isles; and Midlothian and West Lothian. Notwithstanding issues of funding and staffing, the reason for this halting progress was a marked increase in descriptive and illustrative detail. The Commission felt a weight of responsibility to be ever-more comprehensive in the creation of its National Inventory. In effect, striving for completeness meant looking both forwards and backwards. Curle's 1908 survey of Berwickshire in the First Report, for instance, was revised and extended to become, in 1915, the Sixth Report. In 1913, a new Ancient Monuments Act

'In the amplitude and importance of its results, the present survey has far outrun its predecessors.'

An Inventory of the Ancient and Historical Monuments of Roxburghshire (with the Fourteenth Report of the Commission), 1956

offered a much broader definition of what constituted an 'ancient monument'. Changeovers in staffing in the 1920s, '30s and '40s saw substantial redrafts of work-in-progress Inventories, delaying publication dates further. And all the while, developments in professional archaeological theory and practice, along with the implementation of new survey technologies like aerial photography, continued to refine the nature of the Commission's work. Steer even acknowledged, in a progress report to Commissioners in 1953, that his own original assessment of the time required to complete the Marginal Land Survey was 'totally inadequate'. He continued that another five to seven years would be required 'if the scheme is to be carried to its logical conclusion'.

There was a telling line in the introduction to the Fourteenth Report on the county of Roxburghshire, published in 1956

RINGWORK, TORHOUSEKIE

WIG

bracken
DYKE
10 5 0 10 20 30 40 50 FEET.
3"

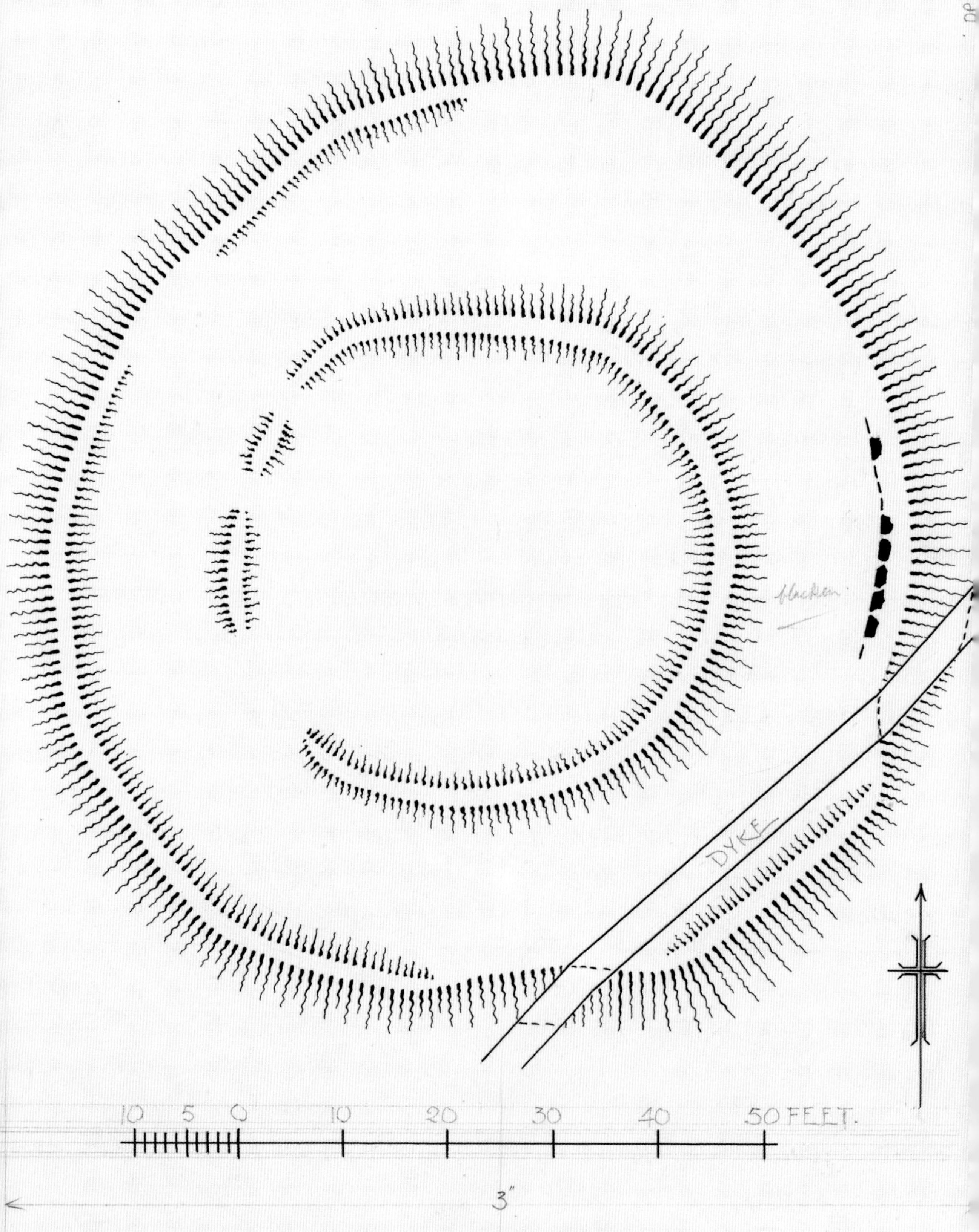

'We have been able to produce an Inventory which is much more nearly complete than any other as yet produced.'

An Inventory of the Ancient and Historical Monuments of Roxburghshire (with the Fourteenth Report of the Commission), 1956

– the first to make substantial and systematic use of aerial imagery in its identification of sites and structures. 'In the amplitude and importance of its results', it explained, 'the present survey has far outrun its predecessors'. As it went on to explain, 'it has been possible to make so full a record of the earthwork monuments, many of which are scarcely visible – or even invisible – to observers on the ground, by means of aerial photographs and the new technique of interpreting them'. The result, said the Commissioners, was 'an Inventory which is much more nearly complete than any other as yet produced'. Implicit in this, of course, was the recognition of the varying, unavoidable deficiencies of the previous thirteen reports – which constituted over half of the survey of Scotland – produced in an earlier era when certain technologies were unavailable. It begged the question: could the task of creating an inventory of the nation ever truly be complete?

Torhousekie, inked plan from Marginal Land Survey c1955. DP149852

The Dynamic Collection

On 1 January 1948, a new Royal Warrant issued by King George VI changed fundamentally the task that the Commission had been set. It was not the nature of the work that was altered, however, it was the scope. The Warrant effectively removed all limitations on what the Commission could include in its inventory. Any site or structure, of whatever date, could be recorded – so long as it was of importance to the cultural heritage of Scotland.

There had been a sense of inevitability about this universal extension. A decade before, on 1 December 1938, the King had given special instructions to the Commission that 'in making an inventory of the Monuments and Constructions in Our Ancient City and Royal Burgh of Edinburgh', it would be permissible to consider buildings dating 'from the year 1707 to the year 1815, as seem to you in your discretion to be worthy of mention'. That this came on the eve of the Second World War was not a coincidence. Advances in flight and weapons technology had placed cities and their architecture in danger like never before. Faced with such an impending threat, it seemed perverse that the Commission's ongoing

Perspective drawing by Basil Spence of the Southern Motors Filling Station, Causewayside, Edinburgh, 1933. DP004289

43

inventory of Edinburgh would not document the extensive Georgian New Town, which had been built after the 1707 cut-off, in the late eighteenth and early nineteenth centuries. But this rationale could never remain logically confined to just one location. It had to encompass all of Scotland. What this meant, of course, was that – as of 1948 – every report that the Commission had so far produced had omitted two centuries' worth of 'Monuments and Constructions'.

'It had become clear that the task upon which the Royal Commission was engaged was neither finite nor quantifiable, taking the form, rather, of a continuous process of assessment driven by society's ever-changing perception of its past.'

John Dunbar, Secretary, 1978–90

There was also one other line in the 1948 Royal Warrant that was to have a huge significance for the future of the Commission. 'We do further authorize and empower you', it stated, 'to confer with the Council of the Scottish National Buildings Record from time to time as may seem expedient to you in order that your deliberations may be assisted by the reports and records in possession of the Council and to make such arrangements for the furtherance of objectives of common interest'. The Scottish National Buildings Record (SNBR) had been established in 1941 with a remit – just like the wartime Commission – to make an emergency record of the nation's historic architecture. The focus of the SNBR was specifically architectural – and was not explicitly restricted by time period. The volunteer staff comprised architectural students and architects, and they created their record predominantly through their own photography and measured surveys. Because of their limited resources, they also made a concerted effort to collect and archive already existing – and often historical – architectural design drawings, as an efficient substitute for carrying out the drafting work themselves. At the outset, there was no official connection between the Commission and the SNBR. It was the 1948 Royal Warrant that made the first tentative suggestion of collaboration. And with the date limit removed from the Commission's remit, the roles and responsibilities of the organisations suddenly overlapped.

Despite this, the Commission and the SNBR continued to work apart for the next decade and a half. In 1962, a Ministerial working group recommended that the National Buildings Records of England and Wales should be brought

North Elevation

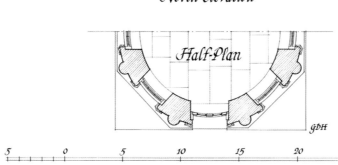

Half-Plan

GDH

5   0   5   10   15   20   25   30 ft.

within their own Royal Commissions. Even then, it took Scotland another four years to follow suit, with the transfer of both archive material and staff – including the Record's redoubtable curator, Kitty Cruft – finally taking place in 1966. The holdings of the SNBR were amalgamated with those of the Commission to create the 'National Monuments Record of Scotland'. Kenneth Steer, who became Commission Secretary in 1957, recognised the significance of the move: 'it has enabled the two largest collections of negatives, photographic prints, and drawings of ancient monuments and historic buildings in Scotland to be combined into a single archive'. It added an entirely new dimension to the National Inventory: a defined collection of physical materials. All of these drawings, plans, photographs, journals and maps had to be collated, curated and cared for. While some would be reproduced in the published Reports – which still remained the focus of the Commission's work – the vast majority would not. It meant that the task at hand had acquired new, and potentially limitless, depths. As John G Dunbar, Secretary from 1978 to 1990, put it, 'In assuming responsibility for the maintenance and development of a major historic archive the Commission for the first time acquired a function that was clearly permanent rather than temporary

The Pineapple, Dunmore Park, north elevation and half-plan, by Commission architect Geoffrey Hay, 1975. DP029783

in nature'. The Inventory, he went on to say, consequently 'came to be construed not as a finite series of published volumes, but as a body of information comprising visual and documentary records of various kinds and having an almost unlimited capacity for expansion and refinement'.

As Dunbar knew, it is inevitable that a 'body of information' will grow – and often at a remarkable rate. At its inception, the National Monuments Record already contained a large amount of historical materials, many of special importance. The National Art Survey – some 1,500 original drawings of Scottish buildings – formed its backbone. Initiated by the renowned Scottish architect, Sir Robert Rowand Anderson, in the 1890s, the Art Survey was intended, as Rowand Anderson himself put it, to 'preserve and perpetuate the best features of Scottish Architecture and educate the

'The inventory increasingly came to be construed not as finite series of published volumes, but as a body of information comprising visual and documentary records of various kinds and having an almost unlimited capacity for expansion and refinement.'

John Dunbar, Secretary, 1978–90

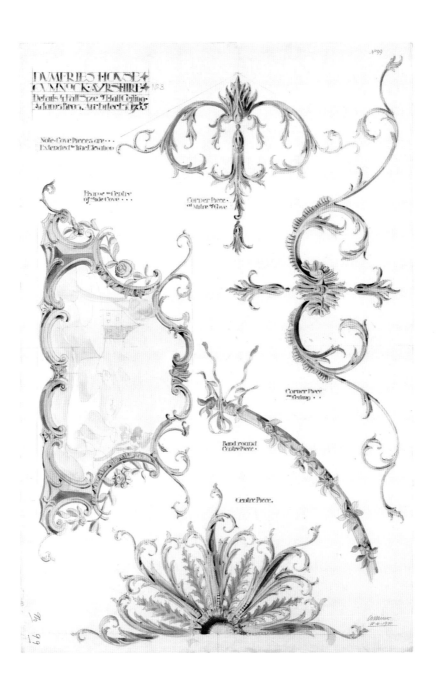

National Art Survey drawing of hall ceiling at Dumfries House, c1900. DP074892

public to a keener appreciation of its interest and beauty'. As a result, the Monuments Record was recognised very quickly as the natural repository for collections and material of significance. In 1968, a large selection of the drawings produced by the early twentieth-century Arts and Crafts architect Sir Robert Lorimer were presented to the Commission. (Ironically, this meant depositing the material in Lorimer's former home of 54 Melville Street – as of 1966, the building had become the Commission's headquarters, and the National Monuments Record was housed in Lorimer's old dining room). The Society of Antiquaries of Scotland deposited part of their Collection documenting research into sites across the country. Historic negatives and image collections joined the many photographs already produced through decades of Commission survey work. The Record soon looked to incorporate printed books as well, seeking out historical and contemporary titles to add to the mix. This was not collecting purely for collecting's sake – Rowand Anderson's ethos of 'educating the public' echoed through the shelves of the new archive. The Monuments Record had a remit to be made accessible and comprehensible, catalogued in such a way that it could be used by anyone to inform and instruct. It was, in effect, a living testament to the special value of the nation's built environment.

The National Monuments Record Library – in Robert Lorimer's former dining room – at 54 Melville Street, 1966. SC357513

Notions of value are, of course, notoriously fluid. Throughout the Commission's history, advances in technology had continually offered new ways of recording and adding to the inventory. Even when the task at hand remained relatively static – structures dating up to 1707 – the prospect of completion was always receding over the horizon. As definitions of cultural importance began to change, however, any sense of an 'end' disappeared completely. Just as the post-war period had endangered archaeological landscapes through large, government-funded infrastructure projects, it also posed a significant threat to architecture. In the 1950s and '60s, huge swathes of historic towns and cities were torn down and replaced with buildings which reflected the modernist tastes of a new generation of architects and planners. Town and County Planning Acts in 1969 and 1972 bolstered the state system for the protection of historic buildings through the 'listing' process – and crucially, presented the Commission with a statutory duty to survey any listed structure threatened with demolition, destruction or alteration. By the late 1970s, this saw some 200 emergency surveys carried out every year throughout Scotland – on buildings from all periods dating up to the Second World War.

Motherwell, Ravenscraig Steelworks. View of open-hearth shop showing charging machine, taken by John R Hume in 1978. SC549419

ORCHARD PARK ESTATE
THORNLIEBANK
4 APARTMENT VILLAS
FITTED WITH ALL LABOUR SAVING
DEVICES AND DECORATED TO
PURCHASERS TASTE FREE
TOTAL DEPOSIT £25
WEEKLY OUTLAY 18/10ᴰ
NO LEGAL FEES — NO ROAD CHARGES
MACTAGGART & MICKEL LTD.
63-65 - BATH STREET - GLASGOW - C.I.
TELEPHONE DOUGLAS ONE

The pace of societal change in the second half of the twentieth century was such, however, that post-war architecture, whose rapid spread had done so much to precipitate the need for 'rescue recording', began itself to disappear. So too, did entire landscapes of heavy industry: coal mines, steel works, railways, docklands and power stations. The result was that the very concept of 'built heritage' had to be radically and rapidly reassessed. The prospect of loss – often of buildings whose significance was still to be appreciated fully – became a constant threat. The Commission reacted by bringing under its roof the Scottish Industrial Archaeology Survey, which had been established in 1977 by future Chairman, John R Hume. In the late 1980s, field investigations were carried out at decommissioned sites like Monktonhall Colliery, Ravenscraig Steelworks and Hunterston 'A' Nuclear Power Station. A decade later, supported by the Heritage Lottery Fund, it embarked on a massive project of salvaging and housing some 200,000 architects' papers, which were in danger of disposal and destruction as firms closed during the recession. From archives of major practices, such as Spence, Glover & Ferguson, to the collections assembled by home-builders like Mactaggart & Mickel, the papers held by the Commission included an incredibly broad

Mactaggart & Mickel original colour advert for
Orchard Park, Glasgow, 1937. SC420817

and diverse record of Scottish buildings in the latter half of the twentieth century. All were recognised as part of the rich fabric of our heritage, and were deemed equally valuable for a national inventory. The work of recording maintained a commitment to objectivity. Throughout the 1990s, for instance, the Commission recorded the slow deterioration and partial eradication of Cumbernauld's 1960s New Town Centre – a place that was simultaneously of international architectural importance, and derided by popular opinion as one of the ugliest excesses of the modernist movement in Scotland. While debate could rage over the need to physically preserve such a site, it was hard to argue against the necessity of recording its existence.

Drawing of Cumbernauld Town Centre by Michael Evans, 1963. SC729363

'It had been assumed in 1908 that the work of compiling a register of Scotland's monuments would be speedily accomplished by one man on a bicycle.'

John Dunbar, Secretary, 1978–90

All of this was a world away from Curle's first investigations of ruins and prehistoric earthworks in the Borders. Except it was not. The Commission's remit had always been to consider structures 'connected with or illustrative of the contemporary culture, civilization and conditions of life of the people of Scotland'. With the date limit removed, it allowed the work of surveying and recording to follow the thread of the national built heritage from Neolithic cairns all the way up to 1960s high-rises; from souterrains to suburban shopping centres. While the techniques and technology behind these constructions may have advanced considerably over the centuries, their uses had barely changed at all: places to live and find shelter; stores for food and resources. It was still the same idea from 1908 that was driving the work. All that had changed was the formal recognition of its true meaning: that when you are recording and archiving for posterity, posterity never remains fixed.

As John Dunbar put it, 'it had been assumed in 1908 that the work of compiling a register of Scotland's monuments would be speedily accomplished by one man on a bicycle. Eighty years later it had become clear that the task upon which the Royal Commission was engaged was neither finite nor quantifiable, taking the form, rather, of a continuous process of assessment driven by society's ever-changing perception of its past'. The dynamic collection was born.

1964 photograph by Henk Snoek of a young boy staring up at Sir Basil Spence's newly completed Hutchesontown tower blocks in the Gorbals. Less than thirty years later, these buildings would be demolished. SC1052310

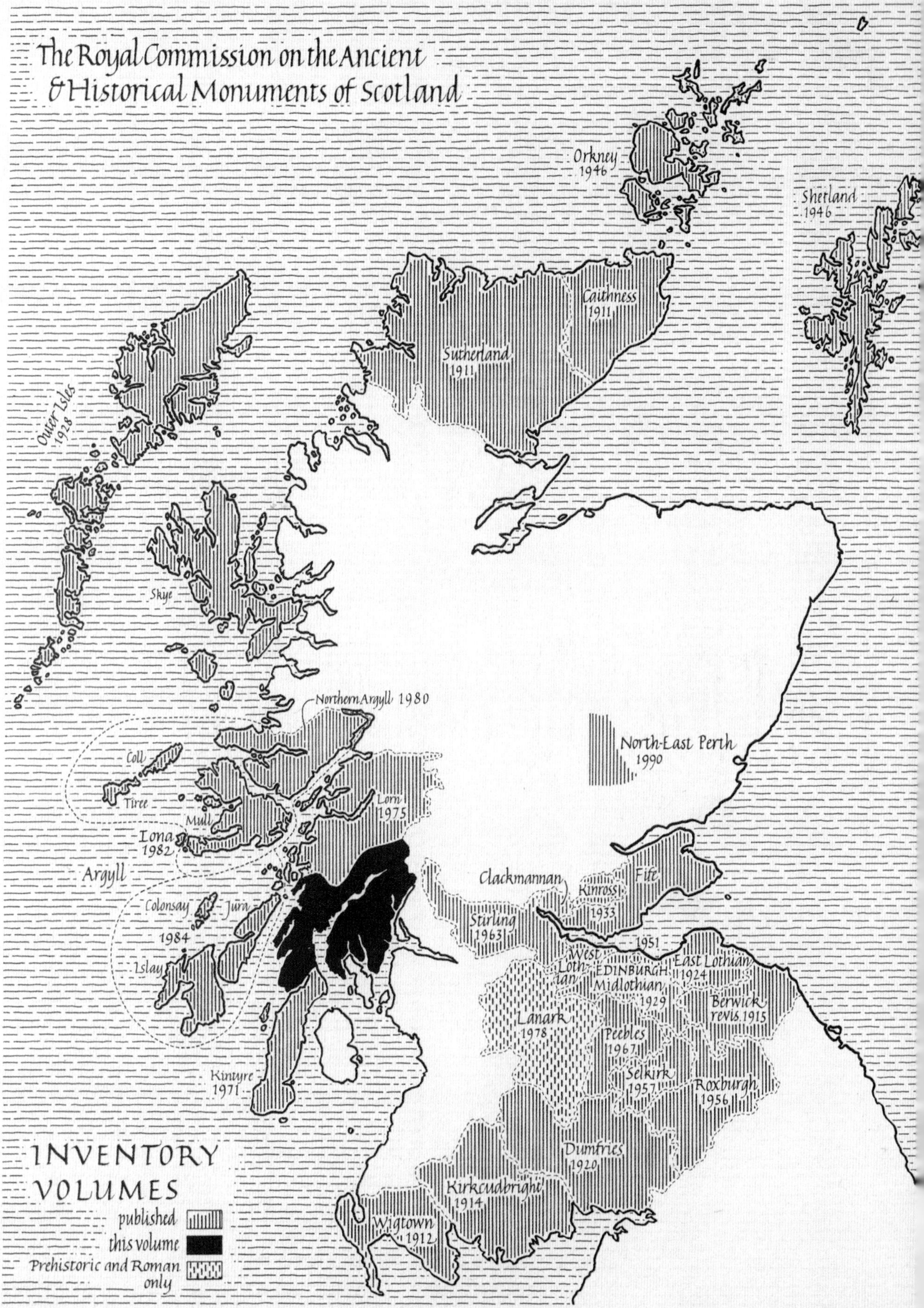

The Royal Commission on the Ancient
& Historical Monuments of Scotland

Orkney
1946

Shetland
1946

Caithness
1911

Sutherland
1911

Outer Isles
1928

Skye

Northern Argyll 1980

North-East Perth
1990

Coll

Tiree

Mull

Lorn
1975

Iona
1982

Argyll

Clackmannan

Kinross
1933

Fife

Colonsay
1984

Jura

Stirling
1963

1951

Islay

West
Loth-
ian

EDINBURGH

East Lothian
1924

Midlothian
1929

Berwick
revis.1915

Lanark
1978

Peebles
1967

Selkirk
1957

Roxburgh
1956

Kintyre
1971

Dumfries
1920

Kirkcudbright
1914

Wigtown
1912

INVENTORY
VOLUMES

published

this volume

Prehistoric and Roman
only

The Information

In February 1992, Roger Mercer, who two years earlier had replaced John Dunbar as Secretary, gave a paper to the Society of Antiquaries of Scotland on 'How the Royal Commission will approach the millennium'. 1992 also marked the publication of the final volume of the Commission's Inventory of Argyll. All of the changes to survey technique, remit and date ranges had led to one of the most detailed works yet produced – possibly in the world – on the archaeology and architecture of a landscape: over 3,000 pages of detailed text, photographs and illustrations split over seven weighty books.

As he looked to the future, Mercer offered an affectionate yet unsentimental assessment of this practice of publishing County Inventories. Acknowledging the Argyll series as the 'zenith of British Royal Commission Inventorisation' he continued that, 'it is already, in very minor details, out of date ... As a monument to the quality of Commission scholarship and endeavour it will stand for many years. But as an itemised record of a specific portion of the heritage of Scotland it will never shine any brighter than on the day it was published'. A modern organisation, anticipating a

Endpaper of the seventh volume of the *Argyll Inventory* showing the Counties of Scotland surveyed by the Inventory series up to 1992, by date.

new century, had to change. 'Published Inventories have not ever really been a practicable, nor, perhaps, a desirable proposition', wrote Mercer. 'By their nature, they seek to define, and as a result they tend to fossilise what must inevitably be a subject of constant reassessment.' Mercer announced that the final volume of Argyll would also be the final Inventory that the Commission published. 'Such a process', he said, 'could not, and will not continue'.

1992 also saw the publication of the Royal Commission's first ever 'Annual Review'. As the Chairman, Robert Alexander Lindsay, the Earl of Crawford and Balcarres, explained in its introduction, the aim was to eliminate 'the irregular timing of Reports' that prefaced the Inventories, and instead, each year 'give a wide-ranging view of the Commission's work in a way which will be more easily available to the general public'. At the same time, the Earl of Crawford and Mercer also provided the official redefinition of the Inventory of the nation. 'In that the National Monuments Record of Scotland is the subject of constant addition, reassessment and development', wrote Mercer, 'it is clear that the basic Inventory that needs to be compiled and maintained by the Commission is the National Monuments Record itself'. The collection had become the Inventory,

'Published Inventories have not ever really been a practicable, nor, perhaps, a desirable proposition … By their nature, they seek to define, and as a result they tend to fossilise what must inevitably be a subject of constant reassessment.'

Roger Mercer, Secretary, 1990–2004

and vice versa. 'It has been designed', wrote the Earl of Crawford, 'to integrate surveying work in the field and accessioning in the Record, with cataloguing and making the material quickly and easily available to the public'.

As Mercer later wrote, this urgent need for the organisation to evolve was driven by 'the most revolutionary developments … in the field of information management'. Reduced to its simplest terms, the Commission's task had always been the gathering, analysis and presentation of information. The latter half of the twentieth century had, however, transformed what this actually meant. As early as 1948, thanks to the American mathematician Claude E Shannon, information had acquired its own discrete unit of measurement: the bit. No longer was it just an abstract concept, it could be valued and quantified. Subsequent decades saw vast and rapid developments in the fields of information theory and information technology – the latter now familiar universally by its acronym, IT. 'The entire business of information creation' wrote Mercer, 'had passed through developmental and exploratory stages in the '70s and '80s, and had raised an irresistible expectation from the wider world'.

'The most revolutionary developments lay in the field of information management.'

Roger Mercer, Secretary, 1990–2004

Running parallel with these technological developments was an explosion in both the ways the Commission went about gathering information, and the sources from which they received it. In 1983, the records of the archaeology division of the Ordnance Survey were transferred in their entirety into the National Monuments Record. Since 1920, the Ordnance Survey, under the auspices of its first Archaeology Officer, O G S Crawford, had been committed, as Crawford himself put it, 'to reduce to order the chaotic mixture of antiquarianism and speculation that disfigured the Ordnance maps and to bring it into conformity with existing knowledge'. It was a task that overlapped considerably with, yet was carried out separately from, the work of the Royal

Commissions in Scotland, England and Wales. Crawford embarked on fieldwork throughout Britain, examining sites and structures, and making his notes in pencil directly onto the 6-inch-to-the-mile county mapsheets. In 1947, his successor C W Philips introduced a series of numbers for archaeological sites, and a card index system, which recorded details specific to each site – including its grid reference, a description of its condition, and a record of who had examined it, and when. These cards were then updated with every new survey, and used as the basis for adding details of ancient monuments to the Ordnance Survey's standard map series, published at scales ranging from 1:2,500 to 1:250,000.

It was not just information alone that was transferred to the Commission by the Ordnance Survey, however. It was also the responsibility for the information's future preservation, revision – and creation. This was a task that brought together everything from archival record management and qualitative analysis to the interpretation and generation of map-based spatial data. Coping with these demands required a revolution in the Commission's own survey techniques, and the increasing adoption of cutting-edge technologies, including Electronic Distance Measuring (EDM) equipment, and satellite-based Global Positioning System (GPS).

New areas of collecting or surveying had continued to develop. In 1976, building on the work of interpreting aerial photography undertaken since the 1930s and '40s, the Commission embarked on its own programme of aerial survey – flying over Scotland and, as the Earl of Crawford put it in the first Annual Review, 'capturing fascinating archaeological information from cropmarks and from the effects of snow and shadow'. Increasingly, these flights looked beyond detecting ancient remains to also include buildings, industrial complexes, townscapes and cityscapes. In 1977, work began on what were termed 'rapid field surveys' to respond to demand for information from local planning and development authorities. Five years later, a major new government forestry scheme – aimed at planting more than 30,000 new acres of trees each year – prompted the creation of a new survey team tasked with carrying out emergency field studies of historic landscapes placed at risk. In 1991, the Secretary of State for Scotland Ian Lang gave the Commission the task of surveying and recording historic shipwrecks within Scottish coastal waters. As Roger Mercer wrote that same year in his first Secretary's Report, 'to the Commission, this opens new doors'. At the same time, he acknowledged that 'such work represents a specialist area of which the Commission at present has no direct experience.

Oblique aerial view of Woden Law centred on the fort, 2000. SC677288

Until it is equipped to deal with this extraordinarily complex area, it can only contemplate holding action ... The data gathering task, the information handling, and most of all, the researching and systemisation of this material demand staff who are fully familiar with the underwater milieu.'

'A stream, soon to become a flood, of information, was pouring into the Commission.'

Diana Murray, Secretary, 2004–15,
Keynote Speech at the Institute for Archaeologists
Annual Conference, 2008

Information cannot help but profilerate. And so the work of collating it, interpreting it and making it accessible can grow in near exponential complexity. As he outlined the 'way forward' for the Commission in 1992, Mercer talked of the need for 'full computerisation of an updated architecture catalogue', 'electronic input of antiquities mapping', 'the ability to open lines of communication ... to allow down-the-line consultation and information exchange' and 'image-processing and image-storage to allow image transmission'. This was the beginning of what he called the 'Big Bang' in the Commission's 'computing'.

Alan Leith carrying out Electronic Distance Measuring (EDM) work at Pitcarmick Barn, Perthshire, 1990. SC370235

As Mercer's successor as Secretary, Diana Murray, explained, 'it became vital to develop information systems to manage the complexities of this, to update it as best we could, and to manage the stream, soon to become a flood, of information, that was pouring into the Commission'.

The block-ship *Nana*, off the coast of Orkney, pictured in 2009. In 1991, the Commission was tasked with recording historic shipwrecks within Scottish waters. DP058591

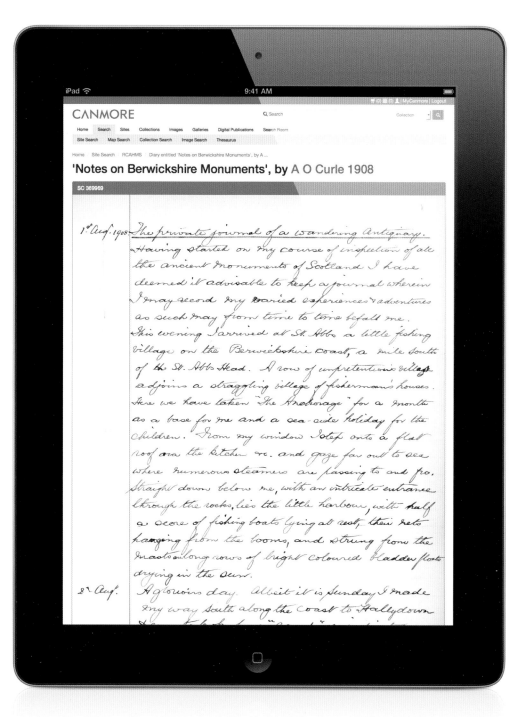

iPad 🛜   9:41 AM

CANMORE

🔍 Search   Collection ▾ 🔍

| Home | Search | Sites | Collections | Images | Galleries | Digital Publications | Search Room |
| Site Search | Map Search | Collection Search | Image Search | Thesaurus |

Home   Site Search   RCAHMS   Diary entitled 'Notes on Berwickshire Monuments', by A ...

'Notes on Berwickshire Monuments', by A O Curle 1908

SC 369969

1ˢᵗ Aug. 1908. The private journal of a wandering Antiquary.

Having started on my course of inspection of all the ancient monuments of Scotland I have deemed it advisable to keep a journal wherein I may record my varied experiences & adventures as such may from time to time befall me.

This evening I arrived at St. Abbs a little fishing village on the Berwickshire coast, a mile south of the St. Abbs Head. A row of unpretentious villas adjoins a straggling village of fisherman's houses. Here we have taken "The Anchorage" for a month as a base for me and a sea-side holiday for the children. From my window I step onto a flat roof over the kitchen &c. and gaze far out to sea where numerous steamers are passing to and fro. Straight down below me, with an intricate entrance through the rocks, lies the little harbour, with half a score of fishing boats lying at rest, their nets hanging from the booms, and strung from the masts along rows of bright coloured bladder floats drying in the sun.

2ⁿᵈ Aug.   A glorious day. Albeit it is Sunday I made my way south along the coast to Hallydown

The Digital Revolution

In April 2015, a group of volunteers working on a project to transcribe some 150,000 pages of historic archive turned their attention to a journal that was over a century old. Every single one of this journal's 182 pages showed the blotches and markings of age. At the top left of the opening page was a date – '1st Aug. 1908' – and alongside it a title, written in an elegant, looping longhand, with a single ruler underline for emphasis. The title read, 'The private journal of a wandering antiquary'. These were the same pages that had recorded Curle's adventures as he pedalled his way around Berwickshire. But they were also pages that, over the last century or so, had undertaken a remarkable journey of their own. Curle's account of beginning the creation of a national inventory had gone from pen to paper to a series of archive shelves in buildings dotted around Edinburgh. Most recently, however, it crossed a discrete physical border. Curle's journal now also exists on the digital plane. Transformed into a mass of binary code – a unique series of ones and zeroes – it is capable of being read by computer processors and reproduced as a 'version' of the original. It is this version that is served up to the volunteer transcribers: available to be read anywhere in the world that has internet access.

A digitised copy of Alexander Curle's diary on Canmore, 2015.

When John Dunbar described the Commission's inventory as 'a body of information comprising visual and documentary records of various kinds and having an almost unlimited capacity for expansion and refinement' he was still thinking in physical – or as some might put it, 'analogue' – terms. What he could not have known was the incredible pace and impact of the digital revolution. Today, for every archive or collection in existence, the capacity for expansion and refinement is now existentially vast. Indeed, a great deal of material is now 'born digital'. In the simplest terms, this equates to an explosion of data. Every day the Commission, through the nature of its work, is creating vast amounts of information and data. And so every day the collection grows

'Archaeological sites and monuments continue to be recorded and classified but, whereas once they were gathered into bound volumes, now they can be delivered via the World Wide Web to remote workstations for interactive use with other datasets.'

Preface, *In the Shadow of Bennachie*, published by the Royal Commission and the Society of Antiquaries of Scotland, 2007

Laser Scan of Coroghan Castle, Canna, 2011. SC1236363

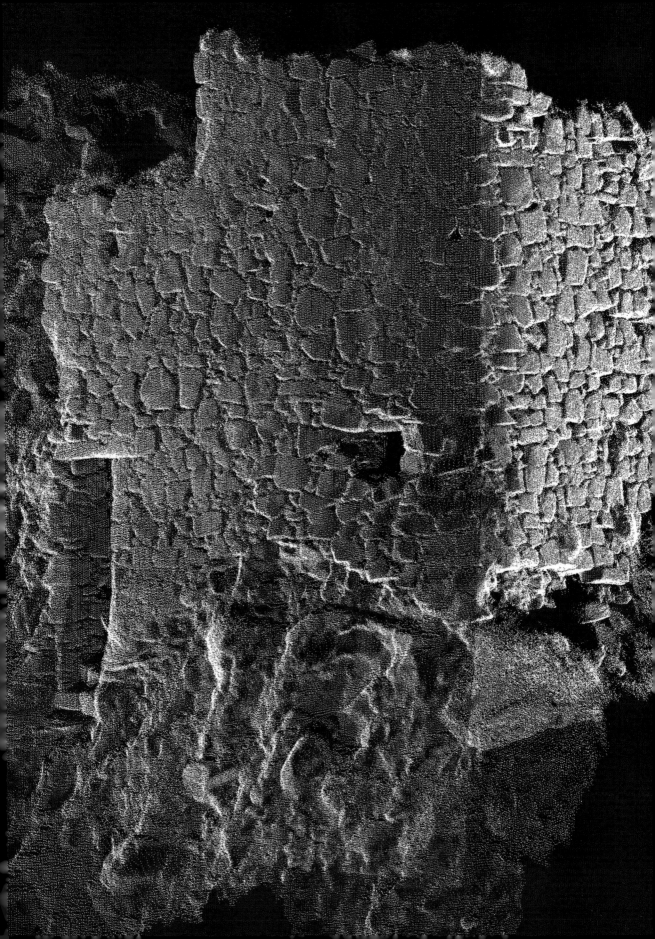

larger and larger. This, of course, presents quite specific challenges. Digital creation is only one half of the task facing a modern archive – the other is digital preservation. The Commission was one of the first organisations in the world to create a computerised system for the management, presentation and preservation of heritage data. Known as 'Canmore', this free online public service provides access to all of the information and research material generated by field survey and recording, and it is the catalogue to the physical and digital archives that are being actively collected and curated. As of 2015, this includes information on 320,000 buildings, sites, structures and monuments, 1.3 million catalogue entries, and 330,000 digital images. Today, Canmore is the National Inventory that Curle and the Commission were first tasked with producing 107 years ago, and it is the 'full computerisation' of the National Monuments Record of Scotland that Roger Mercer predicted. It is the repository of all of the work the organisation has carried out over the course of its history, and as a result of its technical sophistication, it is networked to link information from other heritage data sources, and can be updated instantly as new material and research becomes available. In 2014–15, user searches on Canmore topped five million for the first time – a remarkable testament both to the accessibility of, and interest in, Scotland's national history and heritage.

'We have gone from our very first survey, recorded longhand in a notebook by our first secretary, Alexander Curle, to five million user searches in one year on Canmore, our online database of the built environment. It is a remarkable journey.'

John R Hume, Chairman, 2005–15, and Diana Murray, Secretary, 2004–15

Of course, one of the greatest benefits of digital and web technology is its ability to handle, collate and process huge amounts of information. It has allowed the Commission to take on or digitise vast new collections – including the entire archive of papers, drawings, imagery and correspondence of the architect Sir Basil Spence, and the many millions of aerial wartime and reconnaissance photographs of the National Collection of Aerial Photography (NCAP). It has enabled the development of sophisticated online learning resources, like the Scottish Cultural Resources Access Network (SCRAN) – a web service which joined the

Commission in 2008 – giving the public and education sector direct access to nearly half a million images, films and sounds from museums, galleries, archives and the media. It has also opened up entirely new ways of analysing the built and historic environment. In 1996, the Commission began a project to map digitally every inch of Scotland's landscapes and track how their uses have changed throughout history. This work, which was finally completed in 2015, has drawn on everything from modern and historical Ordnance Survey maps, and the Commission's huge resource of aerial and ground photography, to the records of the Forestry Commission and Scottish Natural Heritage, and staff field surveys. The end result is a digital dataset for all of Scotland served up on a dedicated public website: an invaluable tool for informing decision-making in the use, management and development of land. As a result, in the twenty-first century, the National Inventory has evolved to become a complex synthesis of the physical and the digital. Yet while technology has revolutionised the capacity to gather, collect and organise information, some things remain unchanged. At their very first meeting, the Commissioners decided that assembling data was not enough – if they were to do their job properly, then the organisation would have

The Ring of Brodgar stone circle on Orkney, captured in its wider landscape context on a narrow isthmus between the Loch of Stenness and the Loch of Harray, 2009. DP059208

to interrogate it and create it as well. Today, as the first Berwickshire Report said, it is still 'considered essential' to go on 'personally inspecting each monument as to satisfy your Commissioners as to its true character and condition'. Survey teams continue to operate in the field, visiting and assessing 'Monuments and Constructions' in all corners of Scotland. Just like Curle in 1908, they use their distinctive red and white surveyors' rods, Ordnance Survey maps and tape lines – albeit assisted by Global Positioning System technology to provide incredible accuracy of measurements. When Dunbar began his time with the Commission in 1953 as a junior investigator, he described how, 'if photographs were required, recourse was had to an ancient Sanderson plate-camera, supplemented by a 35mm Leica camera and the Secretary's Rolleiflex'. Flash photography, he continued, 'entailed the employment of generous quantities of magnesium powder, poured into old tobacco-tin lids and distributed at strategic points about the premises. Since the process of ignition was to produce effects reminiscent of an arson attack, this technique was not popular with householders'. Now, cameras offer computer-controlled lenses and light sensors, and memory cards the size of postage stamps capable of holding gigabytes of image data…

'We are looking to the future, and through the diligent and dedicated work of our staff, we can see clearly our place within it.'

John R Hume, Chairman, 2005–15, and Diana Murray, Secretary, 2004–15

Ian Parker taking GPS readings of a cleit during a survey of Borerary on St Kilda in 2010, watched over by curious puffins. DP099635

Yet even this digital photography is far from the cutting-edge. Laser-scanning, for instance, is allowing the creation of exact three-dimensional replicas of buildings and monuments – by firing beams up to 50,000 times a second at objects and surfaces and calculating the distance it takes for them to return. This same technique has been adapted and expanded to record entire landscapes, with survey aeroplanes able to direct lasers down to the earth to record differences in the surface height accurate to centimetres. Just as interpretation of aerial photography in Kenneth Steer's time transformed the ability to detect ancient structures, this process of 'light detection and ranging' (known as LiDAR) is uncovering a remarkable number of previously unknown sites. Every single day, it is possible for the Commission to say that, while 'there are still a number of objects that have not come under our consideration', the inventory of the nation is 'much more nearly complete than any other as yet produced'. 2015 marks the completion of the Commission's Royal Warrant, but not its task. As current Chairman John R Hume, and Secretary Diana Murray, put it, while 'the most recent chapter in the Commission's history is coming to an end, a new one is just about to unfold. On 1 October 2015 all of our work over the last 107 years – along with the work of our partners in Historic Scotland – will continue into a brand-new lead public body … We are taking all of our knowledge, skills and experience and building a new organisation with a new culture, which will help deliver Scotland's first ever strategy for the historic environment. Of course, change has always been a part of who we are and what we do. No organisation can operate for over a century without it. We remain as committed as ever to highlighting the critical role of the historic environment in people's lives. We are looking to the future, and through the diligent and dedicated work of our staff, we can see clearly our place within it.'

In this, our final report, all of those who have worked for the Royal Commission over the last 107 years can echo the words of our first Secretary Alexander Curle. We have inspected all of Scotland. The number of miles tramped – cycled, sailed, driven and flown – we have no reckoning of, but they are many. It has never been anything but the most intense pleasure.

AN INVENTORY FOR THE NATION

A History in Images

Royal Commission architect G P H Watson (middle) follows a local guide out across the shallow waters of Lochlainn on North Uist to inspect Dun Nighean Righ Lochlainn. SC1131201

1924

Robert Adam carrying out an aerial
photographic survey of Glasgow. DP208460

2015

The Royal Commission Land Rover being
winched onto a boat for a survey of
Coll, Argyll and Bute. SC1098516

1967

1947

C S T Calder with survey drawing board on his knee, working inside the remains of Dun An Ruigh Ruadh on the banks of Loch Broom. SC1121381

The 'Scotland's Rural Past' project working with local enthusiasts in Killin. This five-year Heritage Lottery Fund initiative saw Commission experts working with 60 local communities to develop their skills in researching, recording and interpreting historic rural settlements and landscapes.

DP022972

2007

Conservators working on a large drawing from the Sir Basil Spence collection. In 2003, the Spence family presented the Commission with over 40,000 items made up of elements from Sir Basil's personal life, student days, and entire professional career. DP019154

2006

1953

Royal Commission staff and jeep supporting the Scottish Summer School in Archaeology on their visit to Carronbridge Roman fort, Dumfries and Galloway. SC1096824

A *Britain from Above* exhibition at the Lighthouse, Glasgow – just one of the outreach elements of a £1.7 million Heritage Lottery Fund project in partnership with English Heritage and the Welsh Royal Commission, to conserve and digitise the earliest aerial photography collection of Britain and make it publicly accessible. © Peter Sandground

2014

1957

Kitty Cruft, the first curator of the Scottish National Monuments Record, carrying out a photographic survey at Hatton House, Midlothian. SC1098524

Commission staff carrying out a GPS survey of
St Kilda – part of a five-year partnership project
with the National Trust for Scotland to map traces
of human occupation on the islands from early
prehistory right through to the present day

2008

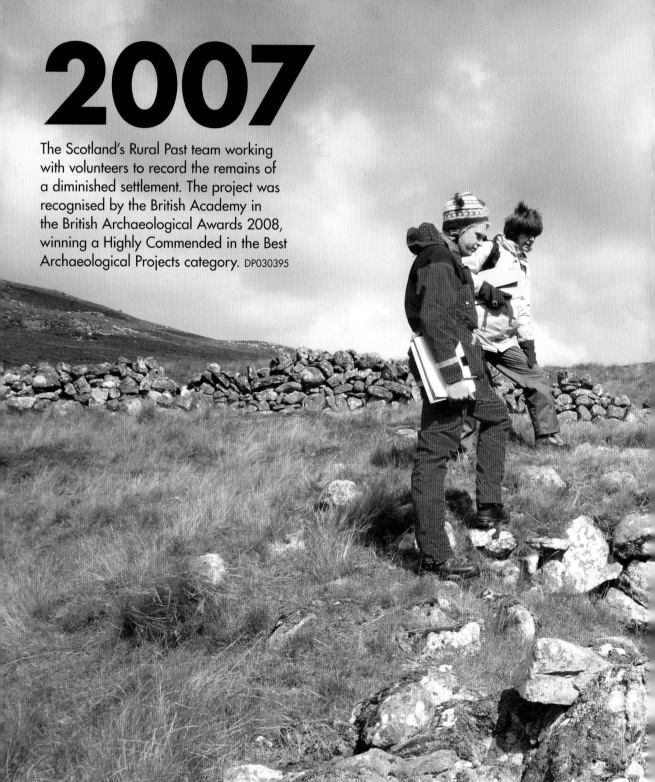

2007

The Scotland's Rural Past team working with volunteers to record the remains of a diminished settlement. The project was recognised by the British Academy in the British Archaeological Awards 2008, winning a Highly Commended in the Best Archaeological Projects category. DP030395

1994

Audrey Wilson, carrying out painstaking conservation work on a rare book. SC371003

Surveyor Ian G Scott and archaeologist Alistair MacLaren in discussion over a plane table at the Dunion, an ancient hill fort near Jedburgh. SC1098663

1961

After nearly five years of expert conservation and cataloguing work by Commission staff, the Sir Basil Spence archive was showcased in 2007–8 in a major exhibition which ran at the National Galleries of Scotland, the Royal Institute of British Architects in London, and the Herbert Gallery in Coventry.

EDUCATION EXHIBITIONS

2008

1966

A Commer van adapted for use as a mobile drawing office for a survey being carried out at Neidpath Castle, near Peebles. SC1096820

John Borland surveying at Lochindorb
Castle in the Highlands. DP206977

2010

Steve Wallace on scaffolding photographing the Phoebe Traquair murals at Mansfield Place Church in Edinburgh. SC556216

2004

1972

Geoffrey B Quick, photographing St
Martin's Cross, Iona. SC1469805

Novelist Alexander McCall Smith
in the search room of John Sinclair House,
researching his book *A Work of Beauty*.
Published by the Commission, the book used
diverse collection material to offer up a unique
history of the city of Edinburgh. DP195531

2014

1966

Sam Scott and Douglas Fleming using tape line to survey the wallhead at Neidpath Castle. SC1096819

Launched to celebrate the Commission's centenary,
the Heritage Lottery Fund 'Treasured Places'
project ran creative workshops and exhibitions
throughout Scotland to help people engage with
Scotland's built heritage. Here schoolchildren
explore the remains of a section of the Antonine
Wall near Falkirk. DP056792

2008

'Skills for the Future' trainee Ruth Macdonald working with material from the National Collection of Aerial Photography. Over five years, the Commission received £900,000 from the Heritage Lottery Fund to provide paid heritage skills training to young people looking for jobs in the sector. DP216613

2012

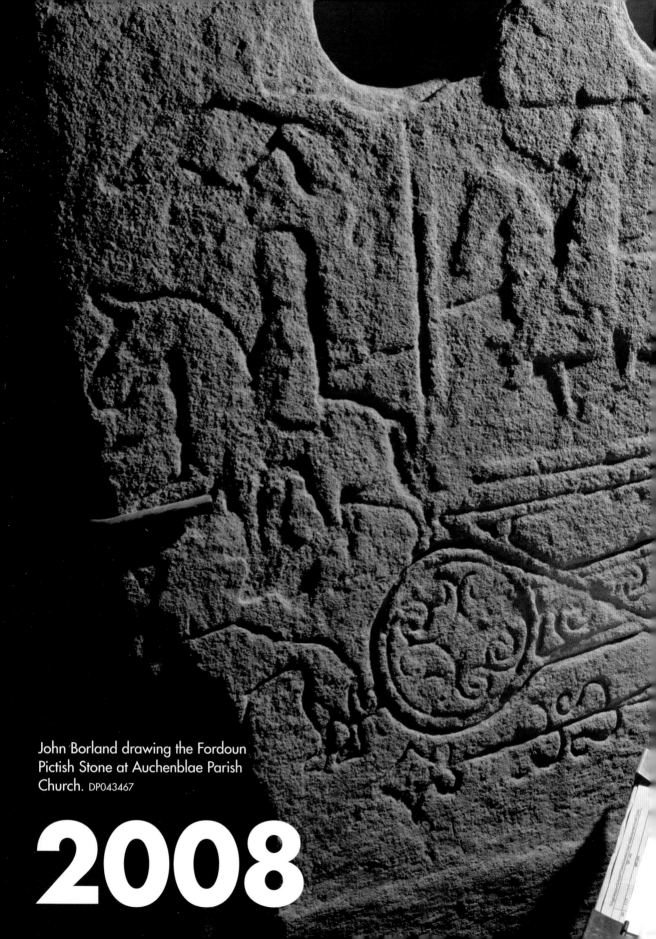

John Borland drawing the Fordoun
Pictish Stone at Auchenblae Parish
Church. DP043467

2008

2014

Two children wearing 3D glasses at Singila
Majengo in Taita Taveta county, Kenya.
The community featured as part of a
Creative Scotland funded documentary
on the international holdings of the National
Collection of Aerial Photography, produced
by the Commission as part of the Cultural
Programme of the Commonwealth Games.
© Noe Mendelle

Angus Lamb and Marilyn Brown preparing for an aerial survey. SC1483915

1990

Tahra Duncan Clark examining the condition of
glass lantern slides awaiting digitisation. DP206978

2013

1987

17

Miles Oglethorpe and Graham Douglas surveying a boiler at the St Rollox railway engineering works at Springburn, Glasgow.

SC1098635

2012

Adam Welfare working on a plane table to produce a measured survey drawing of the Mains of Garten motte, as part of the Cairngorms Community Heritage archaeology project. DP208461

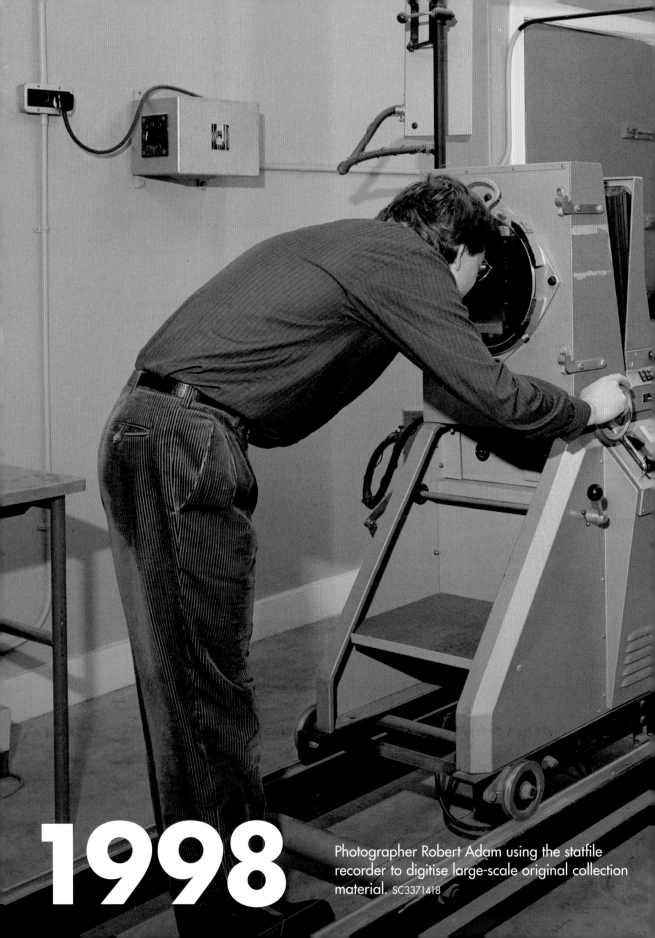

1998

Photographer Robert Adam using the statfile recorder to digitise large-scale original collection material. SC3371418

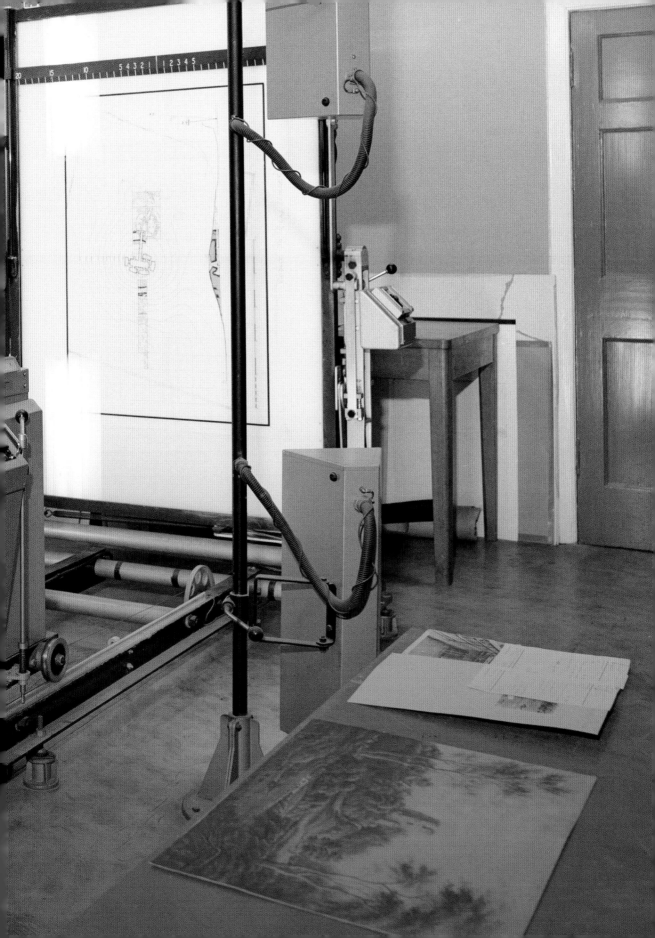

2012

Produced in partnership with Architecture + Design Scotland, and designed by award-winning architectural practice Konishi Gaffney, the *Above Scotland* exhibition showcased some of the best imagery from the Commission's National Collection of Aerial Photography.

2003

A Commission survey team landing on the remote and now uninhabited island of Mingulay, in the Outer Hebrides. SC1154900

An archive image – of the ABC Lothian Road, Edinburgh – on a smartphone is held up against the same site today, as part of the Scotland's Urban Past Project. This £1.65 million Heritage Lottery Fund Project is working with 60 communities across Scotland, giving them the skills to research, investigate, record and tell the stories of the towns and cities in which they live. DP216611

2015

AN INVENTORY FOR THE NATION

Appendices

The Growth of the National Inventory

1908 **1938**

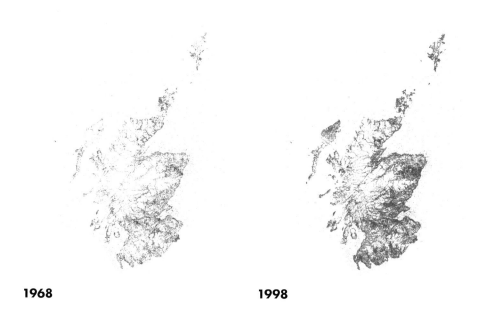

1968 **1998**

Density maps showing how the number of buildings, monuments, archaeological and maritime sites recorded and visited by the Royal Commission has increased over time.

2015

Staff, Budgets and Premises

1908–1913
29 St Andrew's Square

1913–1922
15 Queen Street

1922–1925
4 Drumsheugh Gardens

1925–1931
122 George Street Shared with Office of Works

1931–1946
27 York Place

1946–47
13 Queen Street

ADDRESSES

STAFF NUMBERS

Year	Staff	Annual Budget
1908	3	£600
1909	3	£600
1910	3	£600
1911	3	£600
1912	3	£600
1913	6	£900
1914	6	£1,693
1915	6	£1,693
1916	6	£1,693
1917	6	£1,693
1918	5	£1,693
1919	5	£1,693
1920	4	£2,000
1921	4	£1,500
1922	4	£1,500
1923	4	£1,500
1924	4	£2,360
1925	4	£2,360
1926	4	£2,476
1927	4	£2,518
1928	4	£2,744
1929	4	£2,744
1930	4	£2,494
1931	4	£2,494
1932	4	£2,768
1933	4	£2,689
1934	4	£2,689
1935	6	£2,689
1936	5	£2,603
1937	5	£2,603
1938	5	£2,603
1939	5	£2,600
1940	5	£2,851
1941	5	£2,851
1942	5	£3,035
1943	5	£3,832
1944	5	£5,856
1945	5	£5,856
1946	6	£7,450
1947	6	£7,450
1948	6	£7,905
1949	7	£7,905
1950	7	£8,493
1951	7	£9,388
1952	8	£10,201
1953	9	£10,201
1954	9	£14,570
1955	9	£14,433
1956		£14,433
1957		£14,433

ANNUAL BUDGET

1947–1957
3 South Bridge

1957–1966
7 Coates Gardens

1966–1992
52–54 Melville Street

1972–1992
Also took on external store at 56 Melville Street to accommodate the growing NMRS and provide better public access.

1983–1992
External store at 6–7 Coates Place taken on to house the NMRS as it grew too big for 56 Melville Street.

1992–2015
John Sinclair House 16 Bernard Terrace

External Stores

1994–2015
Causewayside

2006–2011
Baileyfield

2011–2015
Murrayburn

2011–2015
Iron Mountain

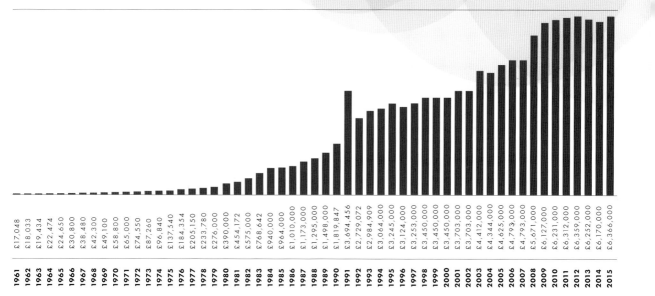

Year	Staff	Budget
1961	10	£17,048
1962	10	£18,033
1963	10	£19,434
1964	13	£22,474
1965	14	£24,650
1966	17	£30,800
1967	21	£38,480
1968	22	£42,300
1969	22	£49,100
1970	22	£58,800
1971	25	£65,000
1972	27	£74,550
1973	27	£87,260
1974	29	£96,840
1975	33	£137,540
1976	33	£184,354
1977	33	£205,150
1978	36	£233,780
1979	36	£276,000
1980	36	£390,000
1981	39	£454,172
1982	39	£575,000
1983	39	£768,642
1984	39	£940,000
1985	39	£964,000
1986	39	£1,010,000
1987	39	£1,173,000
1988	49	£1,295,000
1989	57	£1,498,000
1990	57	£1,819,847
1991	57	£3,694,456
1992	67	£2,729,072
1993	67	£2,984,909
1994	67	£3,064,000
1995	67	£3,245,000
1996	67	£3,124,000
1997	67	£3,253,000
1998	67	£3,450,000
1999	67	£3,450,000
2000	100	£3,450,000
2001	100	£3,703,000
2002	100	£3,703,000
2003	95	£4,412,000
2004	95	£4,344,000
2005	95	£4,625,000
2006	95	£4,793,000
2007	95	£4,793,000
2008	95	£5,671,000
2009	95	£6,127,000
2010	95	£6,231,000
2011	95	£6,312,000
2012	95	£6,359,000
2013	95	£6,252,000
2014	95	£6,170,000
2015	107	£6,366,000

Royal Commission Chairs

Sir Herbert Maxwell
1908–1934

Sir George Macdonald
1934–1940

Sir John Stirling-Maxwell
1940–1949

David Charteris
12th Earl of Wemyss
1949–1985

Robert Lindsay
29th Earl of Crawford
1985–1995

Sir William Fraser
1995–2000

Kathleen Dalyell OBE
2000–2005

Professor John R Hume OBE
2005–2015

Royal Commission Secretaries

Alexander Curle
1908–1913

William Mackay Mackenzie
1913–1935

Angus Graham
1935–1957

Kenneth Steer
1957–1978

John Dunbar
1978–1990

Roger Mercer
1990–2004

Diana Murray
2004–2015

Former Commissioners

The Hon. Lord
Guthrie
1908–1920

Professor G Baldwin
Brown
1908–1932

Professor T H Bryce
1908–1946

F C Buchanan
1908–1920

W T Oldrieve
1908–1922

Dr Thomas Ross
1908–1930

Dr Alexander O Curle
1913–1951

Sir George
MacDonald
1923–1940

Dr James Curle
1925–1944

Viscount Novar
1925–1934

James A Morris
1930–1942

Sir John Stirling
Maxwell
1934–1949

Dr J Graham
Callendar
1934–1938

Sir Iain Colquhoun
1934–1942

Dr Reginald Fairlie
1938–1952

Professor V Gordon
Childe
1942–1946

Dr W Mackay
Mackenzie
1943–1952

Professor V H
Galbraith
1943–1955

Professor Sir Ian A
Richmond
1944–1965

Professor Stuart
Piggott
1946–1976

Dr W Douglas
Simpson
1946–1968

Ian G Lindsay
1951–1966

Professor W Croft
Dickinson
1952–1963

G P H Watson
1952–1959

Dr Annie I Dunlop
1955–1971

Angus Graham
1960–1974

Professor Kenneth H
Jackson
1963–1985

Professor Gordon
Donaldson
1964–1982

Professor P Gordon
Nuttgens
1967–1976

Professor Archibald
A M Duncan
1969–1992

Professor James
Dunbar–Nasmith
1971–1996

Professor Rosemary
Cramp
1974–1999

Dr Howard M Colvin
1976–1989

Professor Leslie
Alcock
1977–1990

Professor George
Jobey
1979–1989

Professor John Butt
1982–1987

Mrs P E Durham
1984–1994

Professor T
Christopher Smout
1986–2001

The Hon. Lord Cullen
1987–1997

James W T Simpson
1996–2006

Dr Margaret
A Mackay
1997–2007

Dr Deborah Howard
1991–1999

Miss Anne C Riches
1995– 2004

The Hon. Peregrine
Moncreiffe
1991–1994

Dr Barbara
E Crawford
1995–2004

Professor John
M Coles
1993–2002

Professor Roland
A Paxton
1993–2002

Professor Angus
MacDonald
1999–2009

Professor Christopher
Morris
1999–2009

Dr Jane Murray
1999–2009

Dr Stana Nenadic
2001–2010

Commissioners 2015

Mr Gordon Masterton
2003–2015

Dr Kate Byrne
2004–2015

Professor John Hunter
2004–2015

Mark Hopton
2007–2015

Elspeth Reid
2008–2015

Tom Dawson
2010–2015

Paul Jardine
2010–2015

Dr Jeremy Huggett
2010–2015

Judith Quartson Mochrie
2010–2015

Exhibitions

Recording Scotland's Heritage
Canongate Tolbooth, Glasgow: July–October 1975

The National Monuments Record of Scotland Jubilee Exhibition
The National Gallery of Scotland, Edinburgh: May–August 1991

Aberdeen Art Gallery and Museum: September–October 1991

Kelvingrove Museum and Art Gallery: Glasgow, November 1991–January 1992

The RIBA Heinz Gallery, Portman Square: London, January–February 1992

Bronze-Age Britain
John Sinclair House, Edinburgh: October–November 1995

St Kilda
Kelvingrove Museum and Art Gallery, Glasgow, 1996

The World of Worship: The Monuments of Christian and non-Christian Scotland
Victoria Quay, Leith: February 2000

St Mungo Museum of Religious Life and Art, Glasgow: February–May 2000

Church of the Holy Rude, Stirling: May 2000

St Salvador's Episcopal Church, Dundee: May–June 2000

Hunter Library and Conference Centre, Restenneth, Forfar: June 2000

St Nicholas' Church, Aberdeen: June–July 2000

Old High Church, Church Hall, Inverness: July 2000

St John's Episcopal Cathedral, Oban: August 2000

Holy Trinity Episcopal Church, Ayr: August–September 2000

Old Parish Church, Peebles: September–October 2000 (end of main tour)

South Leith Parish Church: December 2000

Church of Scotland Offices, 121 George Street, Edinburgh: February–March 2001

Tarbat Discovery Centre, Portmahomack

What Didn't They Build? – 100 Years of the Dick Peddie & Mackay Drawings Collection
RIAS, Edinburgh, July–August 2001

Changing Buildings: Changing Times – The Scottish Architects' Papers Preservation Project
RIAS Gallery, Edinburgh: September–October 2002

From Sketch to Sculpture – The Scottish Architects' Papers Preservation Project
RIAS Gallery, Edinburgh: September–October 2003

100 Houses for 100 European Architects in the Twentieth Century
The Lighthouse, Glasgow, July–August 2003

Back to the Future: Sir Basil Spence 1907–1976
Dean Gallery, Edinburgh: October 2007–February 2008

Royal Institute of British Architects, London: February–April 2008

The Herbert Gallery, Coventry: June–August 2008

Faces and Places
Scottish National Portrait Gallery, Edinburgh: April–July 2008

Treasured Places: 100 Years of RCAHMS
Edinburgh City Art Centre: October 2008–January 2009

**Treasured Places:
Creative Connections**
Adam Smith Theatre,
Kirkcaldy: August–
September 2008

Cromarty Courthouse
Museum: September 2008

Benbecula Airport:
3–29 October 2008

Lanark Library, Lanark:
November 2008

RCAHMS, John Sinclair
House: December 2008

Omni Centre, Edinburgh:
December 2008–January
2009

Dundee Central Library:
January–February 2009

Tweeddale Museum and
Gallery, Peebles:
February–March 2009

The Mall Shopping Centre,
Falkirk: March–April 2009

Moray Art Centre, Findhorn,
Forres: April 2009

The Pier Arts Centre,
Stromness: May 2009

RCAHMS, John Sinclair
House: May–September 2009

**Wanderings with
a Camera – The
Photography of
Erskine Beveridge**
Taigh Chearsabhagh Museum
and Arts Centre, North Uist:
April–June 2009

Scotland's Global Impact
Conference, Inverness:
October 2009

Andrew Carnegie Birthplace
Museum, Dunfermline: March
–May 2010

Scottish Fisheries Museum,
Anstruther: 4 July–5
September 2010

Above Scotland
The Lighthouse, Glasgow:
November 2012–February
2013

Sir Duncan Rice Library,
University of Aberdeen:
February–April 2014

Duff House, Banff:
April–May 2015

Scotland's Lost Gardens
The Royal Botanic
Garden, Edinburgh:
August–September 2013

Sightlines (Film)
Edinburgh International
Film Festival: June 2014

Edinburgh College of Art:
June 2014

The Empire Café, Glasgow:
July–August 2014

The Lighthouse, Glasgow:
August–September 2014

A Tale of Two Cities
(Winner 2014 Arts
and Business Scotland
International Award)

Nanjing Museum, Nanjing,
China: November 2013–
May 2014

Edinburgh Castle: December
2015–February 2016

Britain from Above
Museum of Edinburgh:
February–April 2014

The Lighthouse, Glasgow:
February–April 2014

RAF Museum, Hendon:
February 2014–March 2015

Library of Birmingham:
July–August 2014

Devil's Bridge, Eastriggs:
October–December 2014

Stirling University: 2 April
2015–28 August 2015

Falkirk Past and Present
Howgate Shopping Centre,
Falkirk: June–July 2014

**Antony C Wolffe:
Student Drawings,
1938–1944**
Matthew Architecture Gallery,
Minto House, Edinburgh
College of Art: January 2015

**The Lost Tomb of Robert
the Bruce**
The Hunterian, Glasgow: June
2014–January 2015

Abbotsford House: April–
October 2015

Publications

Royal Commission County Inventories

1909   *First Report and Inventory of Monuments and Constructions in the County of Berwick*

1911   *Second Report and Inventory of Monuments and Constructions in the County of Sutherland*

1911   *Third Report and Inventory of Monuments and Constructions in the County of Caithness*

1912   *Fourth Report and Inventory of Monuments and Constructions in Galloway, Vol.I, County of Wigtown*

1914   *Fifth Report and Inventory of Monuments and Constructions in Galloway, Vol.II, County of the Stewartry of Kirkcudbright*

1915   *Sixth Report and Inventory of Monuments and Constructions in the County of Berwick (Revised Issue)*

1920   *Seventh Report with Inventory of Monuments and Constructions in the County of Dumfries*

1924   *Eighth Report with Inventory of Monuments and Constructions in the County of East Lothian*

1928   *Ninth Report with Inventory of Monuments and Constructions in the Outer Hebrides, Skye and the Small Isles*

1929   *Tenth Report with Inventory of Monuments and Constructions in the Counties of Midlothian and West Lothian*

1933   *Eleventh Report with Inventory of Monuments and Constructions in the Counties of Fife, Kinross and Clackmannan*

1946   *Twelfth Report with an Inventory of the Ancient Monuments of Orkney and Shetland, Vol.I Report & Introduction, Vol.II, Inventory of Orkney, Vol.III, Inventory of Shetland*

1951   *An Inventory of the Ancient and Historical Monuments of the City of Edinburgh* (with the Thirteenth Report of the Commission)

1956   *An Inventory of the Ancient and Historical Monuments of Roxburghshire* (with the Fourteenth Report of the Commission) (2 volumes)

1957   *An Inventory of the Ancient and Historical Monuments of Selkirkshire* (with the Fifteenth Report of the Commission)

1963   *Stirlingshire. An Inventory of the Ancient Monuments* (with the Sixteenth Report of the Commission) (2 volumes)

1967   *Peeblesshire. An Inventory of the Ancient Monuments* (with the Seventeenth Report of the Commission) (2 volumes)

1971   *Argyll. An Inventory of the Ancient Monuments, Vol.I, Kintyre* (with the Eighteenth Report of the Commission)

1975   *Argyll. An Inventory of the Ancient Monuments, Vol. II, Lorn* (with the Nineteenth report of the Commission)

1976–91   *Catalogue of Aerial Photographs* (annual)

1978   *Lanarkshire. An Inventory of the Prehistoric and Roman Monuments*(with the Twentieth Report of the Commission)

1978–88   *Archaeological Sites and Monuments Series*

1980   *Argyll. An Inventory of the Monuments, Vol.III, Mull, Tiree, Coll and Northern Argyll* (excluding the Early Medieval & later monuments of Iona: with the Twenty-first Report of the Commission)

1982   *Argyll. An Inventory of the Monuments, Vol.IV, Iona* (with the Twenty-second Report of the Commission)

1984   *Argyll. An Inventory of the Monuments, Vol.V, Islay, Jura, Colonsay and Oronsay* (with the Twenty-third Report of the Commission)

1988   *Argyll. An Inventory of the Monuments, Vol.VI, Mid Argyll and Cowal Prehistoric and Early Medieval Monuments* (with the Twenty-fourth Report of the Commission)

1992   *Argyll. An Inventory of the Monuments, Vol.VII, Mid-Argyll and Cowal Medieval and Later Monuments* (with the Twenty-fifth Report of the Commission)

Other Publications

1960   *The Stirling Heads. An Account of the Renaissance Wood carvings from the King's Presence Chamber at Stirling Castle*

1972   *National Monuments Record of Scotland, Report 1966–71*

1975   *National Monuments Record of Scotland, Report 1972–74*

1975   *Recording Scotland's Heritage. The Work of the Royal Commission on the Ancient and Historical Monuments of Scotland*

1977   Steer, K A and Bannerman, J W M, *Late Medieval Monumental Sculpture in the West Highlands*

1983   Dunbar, John G and Fisher, I, *Iona*

1985   Baldwin, John R, *Exploring Scotland's Heritage. Lothian and the Borders*

1985   Ritchie, G and Harman, M, *Exploring Scotland's Heritage. Argyll and The Western Isles*

1985   Ritchie, A, *Exploring Scotland's Heritage. Orkney and Shetland*

1985   Stevenson, J B, *Exploring Scotland's Heritage. The Clyde Estuary and Central Region*

1986   Hay, G D and Stell, G P, *Monuments of Industry: an illustrated historical record*

1986   Stell, G, *Exploring Scotland's Heritage. Dumfries and Galloway*

1986   Shepherd, I A G, *Exploring Scotland's Heritage. Grampian*

1986   Brooks, J C, *Exploring Scotland's Heritage. The Highlands*

1987   Walker, B and Ritchie, G, *Exploring Scotland's Heritage*

1988   Harmer, M and Stell, G, *Buildings of St Kilda*

1988   *Tenements & Towers: Glasgow working-class housing 1890-1990*

1990   *North East Perth: An Archaeological Landscape*

1991   *National Monuments Record of Scotland Jubilee: A Guide to the Collections*

1992–95   *Catalogue of Aerial Photographs*

1992   *Dundee on Record: Images of the Past: Photographs and Drawings in the National Monuments Record of Scotland*

1992   *Knoydart: An Archaeological Survey*

1993   *Brick, Tile and Fireclay Industries in Scotland*

1993   *Images of Scotland*

1993   *Strath of Kildonan: An Archaeological Survey*

1993   *Waternish, Skye & Lochalsh District, Highland Region: An Archaeological Survey*

1994   *Braes of Doune: An Archaeological Survey*

1994   *Catalogue of the Scottish Power Collections*

1994   *Colonsay and Oronsay An Inventory of Monuments from Argyll Volume 5*

1994   *Glenesslin, Nithsdale: An Archaeological Survey*

1994   *Pictish Symbol Stones: A Handlist*

1994   *South-East Perth: An Archaeological Landscape*

1994   *Southdean: An Archaeological Survey*

1994   *Surveys of Postwar Buildings*

1994   *Upper Strathnairn, Inverness, Highland Region: An Archaeological Survey, Summary Report*

1995–2007   *Royal Commission Broadsheets (15)*

1995   *Exploring Scotland's Heritage: Aberdeen and North-East Scotland*

1995   *Exploring Scotland's Heritage: Fife, Perthshire and Angus*

1995   *Exploring Scotland's Heritage: Glasgow, Clydeside and Stirling*

1995   Fisher, I, *Iona: A Guide to the Monuments*

1995   *Mar lodge Estate, Grampian: An Archaeological Survey*

1996   Dolan J E, and Oglethorpe, M, *Explosives in the Service of Man: Ardeer and the Nobel Heritage*

1996	*Exploring Scotland's Heritage: Argyll and The Western Isles*
1996	*Exploring Scotland's Heritage: Dumfries and Galloway*
1996	*Exploring Scotland's Heritage: Orkney*
1996	*Tolbooths & Townhouses: Civic Architecture in Scotland to 1833*
1997	*Eastern Dumfriesshire: An Archaeological Landscape*
1997	*Exploring Scotland's Heritage: Shetland*
1997	*Aberdeen on Record: Images of the Past: Photographs and Drawings of the National Monuments Record of Scotland*
1997	*Cardross Seminary: Gillespie, Kidd & Coia and the Architecture of Postwar Catholicism*
1998	*Forts, Farms and Furnaces: Archaeology in the Central Scotland Forest*
1998	*The Sir William Arrol Collection: A Guide to the Scottish Material held in the NMRS*
1998	*The Sir William Arrol Collection: A Guide to the International Material held in the NMRS*
1998	*The Sir Francis Tress Barry Collection*
1998–99	*Scottish Farm Buildings Survey* (3 volumes)

1999	*Scotland from the Air 1939–1949, Volume 1: Catalogue of the Luftwaffe photographs in the National Monuments Record of Scotland*
1999	*Historic Land-use Assessment*
1999	*Home Builders: Mactaggart and Mickel and the Scottish Housebuilding Industry*
1999	*Pictish Symbol Stones: An Illustrated Gazetteer*
1999	*Kilmartin Prehistoric and Early Historic Monuments: An Inventory of the Monuments extracted from Argyll Vol.VI*
1999	*The World of Worship: An Exhibition to Celebrate the Millennium in Scotland*
2000	*Scotland from the Air 1939–1949, Volume 2: Catalogue of the RAF World War Two photographs in the National Monuments Record of Scotland*
2000	*The Historic Landscape of Loch Lomond and the Trossachs*
2001	Fisher, I, *Early Medieval Sculpture in the West Highlands and Islands*
2001	*The Historic Landscape of the Cairngorms*
2001	*'Well Sheltered & Watered': Menstrie glen, a farming landscape near Stirling*
2002	*But the Walls Remained*
2002	*The Historic Land-use Assessment of the Solway*
2003	*Architecture Maps Scotland: Inner Edinburgh*

2003	*The Historic Land-use Assessment of Wester Ross*
2004	*Creating a Future for the Past: The Scottish Architects' Papers Preservation Project*
2004	*Scotland from the Air Volume 3: Catalogue of the RAF Oblique Aerial Photos 1945–49*
2004	*Architecture Maps Scotland: Inner Glasgow*
2005	Hale, A and Sands, R, *Controversy on the Clyde: The Excavation of Dumbuck Crannog*
2006	Glendinning, M and Watters, D, Little Houses, *Little Houses: The National Trust for Scotland's Improvement Scheme for Small Historic Homes*
2006	Oglethorpe, M, *Scottish Collieries: An Inventory of the Scottish Coal Industry in the Nationalised Era*
2007	*In the Shadow of Bennachie: A Field Archaeology of Donside Aberdeenshire*
2008	Ferguson, L, *Treasured Places: A Centenary*
2008	Watters, D, *St. John's Episcopal Church, Edinburgh*
2008	Fraser, I, *The Pictish Symbol Stones of Scotland*
2008	*The Antonine Wall, 1:25,000 Map*
2009	Cowley, D and Crawford, J, *Above Scotland: The National Collection of Aerial Photography*
2009	Ferguson, L, *Wanderings with a Camera in Scotland: The Photography of Erskine Beveridge*
2009	Glendinning, M and Wade Martins, S, *Buildings of the Land: Scotland's Farms 1750–2000*
2010	Crawford, J, Ferguson, L and Watson, K, *Victorian Scotland*
2010	Bailey, R, Crawford, J and Williams, A, *Above Scotland – Cities: The National Collection of Aerial Photography*
2010	Scott, I G, and Ritchie, A, *Pictish and Viking-Age Carvings from Shetland*
2010	Dixon, P, and Hale, A, Mingulay: *Archaeology and Architecture*
2010	Geddes, G and Hale, A, *The Archaeological Landscape of Bute*
2011	Welfare, A, *Great Crowns of Stone: The Recumbent Stone Circles of Scotland*
2011	*The Gargoyles and Cannons of Craigievar Castle*
2011	*Balmerino Abbey: A Cistercian Monastery in Fife*
2012	Crawford, J, *Scotland's Landscapes: The National Collection of Aerial Photography*
2012	Brown, M, *Scotland's Lost Gardens: From the Garden of Eden to the Stewart Palaces*

2014   Crawford, J, Whitaker, K and
            Williams, A, *Aerofilms:*
            A History of Britain from Above
            (in partnership with English
            Heritage and RCAHMW)

2014   Green, S, *Dumfries House: An*
            Architectural Story

2014   McCall Smith, A,
            A Work of Beauty: Alexander
            McCall Smith's Edinburgh

2015   Gannon, A and Geddes, G,
            St Kilda: The Last
            and Outmost Isle

2016   Hunter, J, *The Small Isles*
            (forthcoming)

2016   Dixon, P, Harden, J, Macinnes,
            L, *A History of Scotland's*
            Landscapes (forthcoming)

Royal Commission Chairman, Commissioners and Secretary, September 2015.
Standing (left to right) Dr Jeremy Huggett, Mark Hopton, Jude Quartson-Mochrie,
Paul Jardine, Elspeth Reid, Professor John Hunter, Dr Kate Byrne
and Tom Dawson. Seated (left to right) Diana Murray (Secretary),
John R Hume (Chairman) and Dr Gordon Masterton (Vice-Chairman).

Epilogue

From the Chair, Commissioners and Secretary of the Royal Commission on the Ancient and Historical Monuments of Scotland, September 2015

To the best of their ability and using the extent of their knowledge and experience, the 8 Chairs, 7 Secretaries and 60 Commissioners who have represented the Royal Commission since it was established in 1908, have fulfilled the duties conferred on them by Royal Warrant.

Much has changed since the first Commissioners began their work. New functions have been added. Each generation has developed and evolved how we carry out our survey and recording activity; how we collect and curate our archives; and how we reach out to and engage with the public. New technologies have been adopted. Sites that had not even been built in 1908 are now deemed worthy of recording.

It is clear to us that the activities of the Royal Commission are dynamic and will never be complete. As we hand over to Historic Environment Scotland, we are aware of the challenges that remain:

– Survey and recording must be a continuous process. This is the only way to ensure the quality and currency of information on the historic and built environment.

– At the same time, we must always assess and re-evaluate what should be recorded. Experience has taught us that we must always be open to changing our perception of what constitutes our heritage.

– Prospective survey through remote sensing, aerial survey and ground survey techniques will continually lead to new discoveries.

– The public appetite for participation in recording the historic environment is growing. There is a need to build skills, knowledge and expertise across the widest demographic, working with partners of all different kinds.

– The collection will continue to grow – as it must. No limit can be reasonably placed on its size.

– Delivery of information online through Canmore, the National Inventory of Scotland's Historic Environment, is increasingly important to the public and the call for more digitised content, made more accessible, grows ever louder.

– There is a public expectation that the information delivered through Canmore should be current and reliable. In addition to the daily additions to the content, regular review and overhaul is required.

– Only five per cent of the material we hold in our collection is currently digitised and available online.

– Over the last fourteen years, our efforts to provide suitable accommodation for our internationally important collection have been unsuccessful and the collection is increasingly at risk. Sixty per cent is held in unsuitable conditions.

We hand over our responsibilities to Historic Environment Scotland knowing that much has been achieved and that the Royal Commission is performing its functions to a high level of competence, expertise and skill. We pass on a thriving, dynamic and active collection, but there is still much to do.

We sincerely hope that Historic Environment Scotland will take up the challenge and continue to evolve the work that we have steered for the last 107 years. We wish them well in the task ahead.